If you're looky for
fun, a run, sea, and a
great time away,
this is it!
Enjoy Chris,
Malcolm

The
Cayman Islands
MARATHON
Experience

The Experience Publishers

Malcolm Anderson

First Published 2007

ISBN: 978–0–9683158–3–5

Library and Archives Canada Cataloguing in Publication
Anderson, Malcolm, 1961-
The Cayman Island Marathon experience / Malcolm Anderson.
Includes bibliographical references.
ISBN 978-0-9683158-3-5
1. Anderson, Malcolm, 1961-. 2. Cayman Islands Marathon.
3. Marathon running--Cayman Islands. I. Title.
GV1065.C392A64 2007   796.42'520972921   C2007-904333-X

Published by The Experience Publishers
irn@sympatico.ca
Ontario, Canada
Telephone toll-free: 1-877-755-5155

Cover design by Jacqueline Vinkle
Cover Photographs courtesy of Kelly Holding
and Grand Cayman Marriott Resort

Acknowledgments

This book would not be possible without the interest and support of those that organized and ran in the 2006 Cayman Islands marathon. First, a special thanks to Rhonda Kelly and Sue Greene of Kelly Holding who gave their time and provided photographs and race information. Most importantly perhaps, Kelly Holding put itself 'on the line' so to speak by giving me permission to write the book before the marathon was even run. Many things can go wrong when organizing events such as the marathon. This book is a completely open un-biased account of the Cayman Islands marathon.

The second special thanks goes to the runners, their friends and families, and the volunteers for willingly giving me their time, thoughts and photographs from the marathon, and running more generally. The support has been enthusiastic. I only hope the book does justice to everyone who has contributed. I feel privileged to have shared their insights with you.

I ran the 2006 Cayman Islands marathon. I met some wonderful people, many of whom I've kept in touch with. I give my thanks to you also, for making it such a memorable experience.

From the production side of things I'd like to thank Jacqueline Vinkle for the graphic design work, and Allan Graphics Ltd. for the printing. It's not a book without their skills and design sense.

Finally, there are many others to thank for lots of different reasons that would fill a separate book, but a very special 'thanks' goes to Callum, Jack, Fred, Dave, Gord, Jeff, Donna, Rob, Liz, Shirley, Sherry, Mike, and Karen. Thanks everyone! I hope it's a decent read.

Contents

"So many people, intent on a separate inward commitment, but united in one common physical endeavour. Our motive is private, the context public. We are strangers who are instant comrades."

Kathrine Switzer and Roger Robinson
26.2 Marathon Stories (2006:16)

Chapter 1

Introduction

This book is about the 2006 Cayman Islands Marathon experience. It's a book built around the experiences and stories – the direct words – of the runners, family and friends, volunteers and race organizers.

The marathon distance is 26 miles and 385 yards (42.2 kilometres). That's a long way. Especially at the End.

The Half Marathon distance is also a long distance. Don't be fooled by the 'half' – it is still 13 miles and 192.5 yards (21.1 kilometres). For some runners the half-marathon is their favourite distance. It's long enough to be a serious challenge if you haven't run before, although it doesn't require the same level of training as that for a full marathon.

In a marathon event there is sometimes another option – a relay race over the marathon distance. Here, teams of 4 runners run the marathon. There are less miles to cover for each runner, but still a lot of energy expended on the course.

Running a marathon is not something you just 'decide to do' the night before a race. It takes training, patience and commitment. It requires physical endurance and mental tenacity. It requires good shoes. To finish a marathon is a true accomplishment. For many people it is life changing. It's an amazing feeling to complete a marathon and have a finishers medal placed over your head as you cross the line.

On the morning of Sunday 3rd December 2006, 48 runners completed the Cayman Islands marathon and another 214 finished the half-marathon. In addition, 31 Relay Teams competed with one another. Close to 400 people ran that day. There were runners from the Cayman Islands, the United Kingdom, Europe, Canada, United States, Mexico, South Africa, New Zealand and Australia. Organizers worked around the clock to ensure everything was in place to create a memorable experience for everyone. Over 200 volunteers helped them make it happen.

It was a festive occasion celebrating friendships, achievements and the attainment of personal goals at many different levels.

Above all else it was a lot fun.

In 1896 the winner of the first modern day Olympic marathon finished in a time of just under 3 hours (2:58.50). The course was approximately 25 miles from the Village of Marathon into Athens, Greece. Hence the name of the race, which has stuck – 'Marathon'.

One hundred and ten years later, over a distance of 26.2 miles (the now standard marathon distance), and on the other side of the world, the winner of the Cayman Islands marathon finished in a time of just over 3 hours (3:06:17).

Marathon running has come a long way in 110 years.

The Cayman Islands

The Cayman Islands are located in the western Caribbean about 150 miles south of Cuba and 480 miles south of Miami. The islands are low lying and surrounded by coral reefs.

Total land area of the islands is only 100 square miles. The largest island – Grand Cayman – is about 22 miles long and eight miles at its maximum width.

It's a 70-minute flight to the Cayman Islands from Miami. As one travel book notes "The Cayman Islands are a stress-free haven, framed by deep blue skies, twinkling sea and golden sand".

It is a tropical paradise. And not a bad place to go for a run.

Thousands of people run marathons every year. Over 800 marathons are run somewhere around the world annually. What makes the Cayman Islands marathon attractive to many people is that they can combine a vacation with running. It's a perfect example of a Destination Marathon. If you love travelling and enjoy running, the Cayman Islands marathon may be the experience for you.

But the weekend isn't just about visitors coming to the Cayman Islands to run a marathon. There are many local runners also competing. There is, in fact, a vibrant running community in the Caymans.

This story of the Cayman Islands marathon experience starts with information about marathons in general. What are they? Why do people run them? What do they do to us? And who runs marathons? It turns out – as we'll see in the book – that all sorts of people run marathons.

As context is always important, the book also devotes a few pages to the history and current context of the Cayman Islands. Most of the book, however, describes the Cayman Islands marathon experience – the race history, the organization and logistics involved in setting it up, and the experiences of the runners and volunteers on the day. The book finishes with a brief look at other attractions in the Cayman Islands. This is a Destination Marathon after all.

As author, I've tried to weave the weekend together based on interviews, and the stories and photographs sent to me by runners, friends and volunteers. I hope the integration of stories and narrative makes this an interesting book to read.

And so at 5am, filled with a range of emotions and preparedness, the runners set off in the humid Caribbean darkness from the Breezes by the Bay intersection in George Town. By the end of the morning it was all over, but the memories will remain for years to come.

What's so special about running a Marathon?

Our fuel for running is carbohydrates. The human body typically has enough carbohydrates to endure a distance of 32 kilometres. The marathon distance is 42 kilometres, leaving us with 10 kilometres (6 miles) of what Tim Noakes in his book The Lore of Running calls the 'physical no-man's-land'.

This is where the challenges come from the marathon distance. It's where training is essential. Tim Noakes describes it this way:

"It is at that stage, as the limits to human running endurance are approached, that the marathon ceases to be a physical event. It is there that you, the runner, discover the basis for the ancient proverb: "When you have gone so far that you cannot manage one more step, then you have gone half the distance that you are capable of". It is there that you learn something about yourself and your view of life. Marathon runners have termed it the wall."

You will take somewhere between 30,000 and 50,000 steps to run a marathon. Over that period carbohydrates, which are found as glycogen in the muscles and liver and as glucose in the blood, get used up. Your muscles get their energy from the glucose and the glycogen. You hit the wall, or 'bonk', when the glycogen levels become depleted. With no 'fuel' left the body then resorts to using slower-burning fats. You'll notice a substantial change in your running speed and it is here that the mind faces the challenges. It is this that makes the marathon what it is.

But with proper training your body can improve the way it burns its fuel and it can push the wall further and further out – ideally enabling it to avoid hitting the wall completely.

Chapter 2

Why Run?

Ask a runner why she runs and there is likely to be a long list of reasons given to you. The reasons may not always be the same from one person to another, but some reasons are consistently stated.

In their spectacular book '26.2 Marathon Stories' Kathrine Switzer and Roger Robinson list the many benefits that scientific evidence attributes to running. It goes like this: Running ...

- Strengthens the heart and reduces the rate of heart disease.

- Enhances creativity and problem solving by stimulating endorphins.

- Improves sexuality by maintaining strong blood flow and creating a positive self-image.

- Helps maintain (or create) healthy sleep patterns by leaving your body fulfilled and tired.

- Reduces the incidence of many forms of cancer by pumping oxygen and antioxidants through your body, which fight against carcinogenic free radicals.

- Reduces toxins in your body by evacuating waste promptly.

- Burns out infection by raising body temperature to fever level on a daily basis.

- Eliminates toxins through the skin and air by stimulating sweating and increasing breathing exchange.

- Pushes disease-fighting white blood cells and immune substances through your system with the release of adrenaline.

- Reduces stress on the heart, joints, lungs and muscles and non-insulin dependent diabetes, by reducing weight and countering obesity.

- Reduces stress by stimulating endorphins.

- Counters depression by stimulating endorphins.

- Reduces the incidence of osteoporosis by strengthening bones.

If that's not enough, experts on aging note that running increases longevity and improves the quality of later life.

The non-science attributes are just as supportive. There is an amazing spirit associated with runners. It's well known that distance runners and walkers are a very friendly social bunch of folks. Runners come together with a common goal, but behind the scenes, especially with marathons, there are remarkable stories of courage, perseverance, resolve, tenacity, dedication, commitment – the list goes on. There are many wonderful people to meet and share experiences with. Comraderie and common purpose coalesce.

There are inspirational stories around the world.

John Stanton, the man who started The Running Room chain of stores, said he was once an overweight food executive who smoked two packs of cigarettes a day. He went on a short fun run with one of his children and got hooked. He hasn't looked back.

In 1983 **Gina Little** saw the London marathon go past her street. She thought 'I could do that' and started training. She only ever intended to run one marathon but got the bug. Now, with over 240 marathons to her name, she has run more marathons than any other woman in the United Kingdom.

Bob Dolphin, who has now run over 400 marathons, said his car wouldn't start one morning so he walked 2 miles to work. He enjoyed the walk immensely, so he kept on walking to and from work. At 48 years of age he started running. He decided to run to work and back each day. He ran his first marathon at age 52. Now at age 77 he has his sights set on 500 marathons. Inspirational.

John Dawson had a heart attack in 1991. It changed his life. He took up running and has not stopped. He has now run over 230 marathons. In May 2007 he was one of eight runners who ran 10 marathons in 10 consecutive days, and by so doing entered the Guinness Book of World Records. John turns 70 in 2007. In the latest London UK marathon John trained, and then ran with, a boy who has Down's Syndrome, enabling this boy to run in the marathon. John is an inspiration to everyone who knows him.

John Wallace, a school caretaker in London England, turned 50 in 2007. He registers for each marathon as Clark Kent and runs in a Superman costume. He has run over 240 marathons and in doing so, has also raised $100,000 for charities.

These marathoners are not elite runners. They are like you and I. They set goals. They have a passion for running and do it for enjoyment and all the other benefits that running offers.

Taken all together, running marathons can be quite addictive.

In some ways running a marathon may seem to be an unattainable goal. Well it is unattainable if you don't train, but that's the point. I couldn't go out tomorrow and run a marathon without having trained. You can't cheat. Sure, you can try, but it's going to really hurt.

The distance is such that if you haven't trained, your body will say 'I don't think so'. It may do so even if you have trained. You may hit the wall. It's as if someone has just put your body in a vice and squeezed out any energy you had left. With no energy left everything seems to be a struggle until the end of the run. Mentally you may not be with it either, and start to question what you're doing. To some people this is called character building. To others it's simply a nightmare come alive.

If you've never run before, just running to the end of the driveway may be your first goal. Or perhaps going for progressively longer and longer walks. After a while you may want to try a bit of running. And then some more running. You may want to alternate running and walking. You might go out in the car and see how far it was that you ran for 15 minutes. You're starting to get hooked at this point.

A great way of starting is to try run/walk programs and build up your stamina by integrating the two. The distance you cover will increase as your body gets used to the idea. Soon, you may decide to enter a 5 or 10-km run. These are a lot of fun. And so it goes ... and you keep looking to the next possibility.

There are many training books out there that say the same thing – take the small steps to larger goals, be patient and stay committed. Completing a half-marathon or marathon at the end of a few months of training is one of those life changing moments, and it's possible for almost anyone if they want to make it happen. Making it happen in the Cayman Islands just adds to the enjoyment.

The runners who came to the Cayman Islands for the marathon had their own reasons for why they run. Here's what some of them said:

For over 20 years I have been experiencing the pleasure and the PAIN of long distance running. I am fortunate enough to have the support of my FAMILY & friends who have motivated and encouraged me every step of the way.

"This was my first half marathon ever. I didn't know if I could do it and didn't know if I couldn't do it, and since I'm just crazy (stubborn?) enough to think that trying something like this, with very little training, would be something "fun" to do, the only option available to me was to try one on for size. I enjoyed it so much, that I'm signing up for the Cayman Islands Cancer Society's Half Marathon in January 2007."

"Running half-marathons (and many other distances) is a long term strategy to offset health risk issues, in my case family history of cardiac disease at early age. My intent is to stay active as long as possible and enjoy a high quality of life. With this in mind I have been running and engaged in other cross-training activities for 25 years."

" A 4 hour RUN is a great way of getting a thirst! "

"The feeling of accomplishment is simply unrivalled by anything I have ever done in my life - it is just you against the elements. It is "Mind over matter - if you don't mind, then it don't matter! Just KEEP running!!""

Achieving Goals

This was the second marathon I ran last year. I ran them for a number of reasons. First it has been a goal for me since I was a child. I've also felt I've been gaining weight slowly over the past ten years. My health habits have also been deteriorating for the same time. Setting large goals for myself seems to be the only way I respond. Not to mention once I ran my first half marathon I was hooked. Then in September I ran the Indianapolis marathon and it was the one of the most emotional experiences I have ever had. I hope to continue to run them for my health.

I run for the sheer **CHALLENGE** of it (I also **Love food** and this way I can **eat** whatever I like and it **doesn't matter!!!**)

"I might as well tell ya, I'm not much of a runner. Cycling and triathlons are my passion, but during the winter months there are not a lot of triathlons happening so I run in a few half marathons in order to keep my fitness and training motivation up. Travel is another passion, so anytime I find a race in a great location I am always eager to sign up."

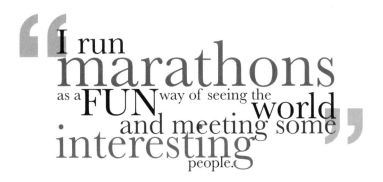

I run marathons as a FUN way of seeing the world and meeting some interesting people.

"I have always watched and talked to marathon runners and had great admiration for their achievement. Watching people from all walks of life, and completely different age spans, attaining such a momentous feat makes me feel proud and I want to emulate them."

I enjoy the simplicity of running and the challenge of COMPLETING a relatively long distance.

> ## "I Love it!
> I think you either
> hate or LOVE RUNNING,
> and I love it!"

Running to Learn

I have been running marathons since 1982. I run them because through running I have learnt about myself at the deepest level. Running has been a constant theme in my life and from a little girl all I have ever wanted to do is run. I have run through sad times and happy times and had triumphs and bitter disappointments, but I have ultimately learnt that I am not a better person if I succeed or a lesser person when I fail, I am just me, living my life - and in learning to run - (and after more than 40 years of running I am still learning to run!) I have found that in truth I have been running to learn - to learn about me, to learn about life, to learn how to live better. So round I go, still running, still unravelling and in each cycle I understand more and see more and grow more. My desire is as high as when I was young, but I am free of the fear - I am free of the pressure that I was somehow trying to earn love and approval through being a great runner - and I was fast - 2.36 at my best - but interestingly I found how loved I really was when I had to pull out of the Commonwealth Games marathon at 20 miles in 1986 - and ultimately through all the trials and tribulations I have learnt to love me and at last free myself to simply run because I love to run.

Chapter 3

Training for a Marathon

Although many people feel that finishing a marathon is either extremely difficult or impossible, many runners and coaches believe it's possible for almost anyone prepared to put the time into training.

All the training programs on the Internet or in books recommend building up your capacity to run slowly over many weeks or months. Over time you'll find that it gets easier and easier. Patience really is a virtue.

It makes a lot of sense to start with run/walk programs. More and more marathoners are using these programs. There is a growing realization that breaking up the running with walk breaks will be less stressful on your body, will reduce chances of injury and will ensure you have plenty of energy to finish the race and enjoy it. Ultimately the choice is yours as to how you'd like to train and run a marathon.

A typical training program will include smaller runs during the week and 'the long run' in the weekend. The smaller runs may or may not include hills. The long run gets progressively longer over the duration of the training program – to such a point that by the time of the marathon you will have already run (or run/walked) up to 20 miles.

Maybe more. The important thing is to build incrementally and not to try too much distance too soon. The risk of injury rises considerably if you do not build up slowly.

For those of us just looking to finish a marathon, a minimum of 3-4 months of running 4-6 days a week is usually recommended. Many programs will advocate an increase in mileage each week of no more than 10%.

As much as you may like to push ahead when you feel some pain during a training program, it's important to take a break and rest the various parts of your body that may be a problem. The most common injuries occur with muscles strains, the knee, Achilles tendon and shin splints. Good shoes make a huge difference.

There's no point in trying to be a hero in training. The more you injure yourself the less likely you'll run the marathon. Let your body heal. In fact, overtraining can occur if you don't give your body enough time to recover. As well as increased risk of injury, you'll find that if you've over-trained, your speed and endurance will also suffer.

Tapering

Another important part of the training is the taper – most commonly done in the last 2-3 weeks before the race. In this period, there are more rest periods and the distance you run is dropped substantially. Tapering helps your body to get into as optimal a condition as possible for the marathon itself. It's a strange time as you may be itching to run. But training programs consistently state that it doesn't matter if you put the same or more training into the last couple of weeks because it will make little difference to your performance and may only increase the risk of injury.

A challenge with tapering is that you are no longer doing the exercise you've become accustomed to, but yet you may still want to keep eating. You may gain a little weight actually, but don't worry; that's not unusual. Diet and nutrition are other important aspects of training to consider but there's not the space to discuss these in this book.

A common practice in the last few days before a marathon is to carbo-load. This will help to store glycogen. Glycogen is that sugar-like substance we introduced in Chapter 1 that is the primary fuel our muscles use when we exercise. But to reiterate once more, the carbohydrates we eat are converted by the liver and muscles into glycogen. Once we've used up all our glycogen over long distances our body turns to burning fat. To some people this probably sounds quite desirable but it's not an efficient fuel source and isn't a great feeling on the run.

In her book on sports nutrition Nancy Clark points out that the biochemical changes that occur when you train affect how much glycogen can be stored in your muscles. Studies have shown that well-trained muscles are able to store between 20% to 50% more glycogen than untrained muscles.

When your glycogen stores are depleted you hit that wall – named so because that's how it feels, and it happens quite suddenly!

You really don't want that feeling, which is why you train smart and develop your muscles so that they can store more glycogen. And the whole idea of running long slow training runs is to get your body used to using its fuel more efficiently in order to conserve glycogen stores. The more and longer these long training runs are, the less likely you will hit the wall.

Here's what some of the Cayman Islands marathoners said about their own training:

Training for the Half Marathon • Part 1

After hearing about the Cayman Islands Marathon in the local press, I decided towards the end of September to run the half marathon. I had no idea where to begin so I researched online, found a few training guides and chose one for "novices", since all the other ones said "advanced", and seemed more geared to elite runners. I planned for 12 – 16 weeks of training. However, Dec 3rd was only 8 weeks away, so I just started "plunk" in the middle of the plan and added a mile or so to the recommended mileage each time as I figured I was somewhere around intermediate. Although I was already running a few times a week, I started training on Oct 1st but did not get the courage to absolutely commit until towards the end of October after I had started to run more miles and so felt that perhaps I actually could run the distance without passing out.

I would train on my own in the mornings (at 5am! in the dark!). With an active family this was the only time that I could find for myself to ensure that I put the necessary miles in. Many mornings I ran exhausted from lack of sleep or from an exhausting squash match the evening before. So often I hit the snooze button before finally getting up that my husband doesn't even hear the alarm anymore – he is immune to it! During my first long run of 9 miles I wondered what I had let myself in for as I slowly dragged myself home picturing glasses of ice cold water and imagining myself in the pool at the end. I told myself that I couldn't do this, it was impossible, but of course by this time I had already registered so there was no turning back. The next week nine miles was much easier and each week as the distance built I felt more confident that I could complete the distance. Although I timed all my runs, I did not really check the pace. My training goal was to get the miles in but my race day goal however was to break 2 hours, so I figured just under 9 minutes per mile would do it. I wanted to run a good time but also enjoy the race and keep at a comfortable pace throughout so that I could enjoy it.

Commitment

It must feel good to be fit enough to run 26 miles. Like lots of people, for years I have been thinking one day I will run a marathon. I began running in March 2006 just for fitness. I had jogged for fitness before but not run a race since cross-country at school. My fourth child was almost one year old, my fortieth birthday just one year away. I could barely run to the end of our street, just 400-yards. I wanted to lose the extra 10-lbs of baby fat and regain some energy that sleepless nights and breastfeeding had drained. Around June I heard about the Cayman Islands Marathon, I checked on the date and made the half marathon my goal. I could spare enough time from work and the children to train. I made my training a priority and I bought a book " How to Run a Half marathon You Can Do It" by Jeff Galloway, which helped with training schedules and motivation tips, my favourite being, reward yourself by buying something nice if you complete your long run. Unfortunately 6 weeks before the race, my mother died suddenly, a complication of the chemotherapy she was taking for her breast cancer. I continued training though my endurance was significantly reduced, because of all the stress my body was under. The running helped to relieve the stress and gave me time to myself to think. It helped me cope better with the grieving process. Just before the day I was quite nervous. I hadn't been able to do as many long runs as my schedule had suggested, 10.4 miles being my longest and that had been 6 weeks previously. I was anxious about not being able to complete the 13 miles. But on the day of the race, despite a very restless night, not trusting my alarm clock to go off, I felt ready.

Start out slowly and build up your endurance. Give it your best effort and even if you don't make it through, nobody, and I mean nobody can fault you for trying. Oh, and make sure that your footwear is comfortable and broken in. The running shoes I wore were about 1/2 a size too small – my feet fit into the shoes well enough, but there wasn't enough space at the toe to provide adequate movement and prevent blisters.

"Wear good shoes and wear appropriate clothing. There is no substitute for training. If you want to finish, run long (18-22 miles) a couple times 3-6 weeks out. If you want to run fast(er), include a speed workout of 4-6 miles at least once a week for a few weeks."

Roger MacMillan | Running the GalloWay

At age 69, Roger was the oldest competitor running in the Cayman Islands marathon. He's originally from the United Kingdom but now lives in Alberta, Canada. He started running in 1989 after asking a fellow worker one day where he got all the running shirts he was wearing. His co-worker said from the running races, and this spurred Roger on to register for a 10km race. He found the training groove and got addicted to the running like many others. Since that time he has run 35 half-marathons and a full marathon.

Roger is fortunate in that he has 15km of trails almost right at his doorstep in Fort Saskatchewan where he lives. But in a Canadian winter training can be very challenging. As Roger explained, being as far north as he is in Northern Alberta, it's great if you can do some of the training indoors. "I did most of my training on an indoor track in The Northwest

Territories just 200 kilometres south of the Arctic Circle. I have been doing some work up there and for the past 10 weeks or so could not go outside due to the snow, winds and cold weather (down to minus 35 degrees Celsius, with the wind-chill)." Three laps of the indoor track would be one kilometer, and five would give you a mile.

"Prior to those few weeks I had been training and running at home in Fort Saskatchewan, Alberta and ran in 2 half marathons there, and one in the North of England, "The Great North Run". That is the world's biggest half marathon and has 50,000 runners, coincidentally my time in that race was only 6 seconds different from my time in Cayman's Race."

Roger used Jeff Galloway's 10 and 1 programme – run 10 minutes and walk 1 minute. He says "It is the best programme I have ever seen. He has also written the best book on Marathon running, titled "The Marathon You can do it". He has a website runinjuryfree.com, with marathon training schedules for all levels, even people who have never ran before. And all of them use the run and walk technique. I used the programme to run the Vancouver Marathon last May and it really works great."

Roger says he runs for several reasons. These include keeping fit and living longer, preventing bad habits from creeping into your life, the enjoyment of it, fresh air and being able to get out amongst nature and hear and see the birds and wildlife. As he put it "You see things you don't see when you are driving". To Roger it's also about the comraderie of running.

And although it's great to try and beat your best times, it's much more about the enjoyment of the run itself. Roger's advice for potential runners is that "you've got to want to do it". He adds, "Start slow – with small distances and build up using the run-walk approach. Leave the ego at the door. If you've got to walk, walk". He said one of the hardest things to do is convince good runners to walk. Another good way to get into running is to get inspired by reading stories of others. In this year's Cayman Islands half-marathon Roger's time was 2:08.

The day before the race the runners go to registration, pick up their race package (including their bib with race number), a goody bag (with instructions on starting procedures, bag drop-off etc and maybe some treats or even gifts) and the expected, and much anticipated race T-shirt.

The evening before the race there is the traditional pasta party. The tradition is based on the fact that pasta will assist in the carbo-loading process, but it's typically not the only thing available at a pasta party. It's also a great opportunity to meet fellow runners and to hear more about the race.

The night before the race the runners may set out their gear for the next day, fasten their bib on their shirt and make any other last minute preparations to avoid potential race-day angst. There's a good chance they may not sleep that well the night before the race; thinking about the day to come.

And then there's race day.

The books and programs provide advice on what to eat before the run, and make suggestions for what to drink and possibly eat during the run itself. It's a really good idea to experiment with which drinks and foods work best during your training before trying these in the marathon itself. The last thing a runner wants to do is increase their mileage and time continuously running to the nearest porta-potty. And they won't want to stand there waiting for one to become available either.

If there are no porta-potties around you'll find that runners' inhibitions are much less than the general public's, perhaps through sheer necessity, and they'll do what they need to do in the most appropriate place possible. They don't really want to be thinking about 'that kind of stuff' while running, so knowing what works during training is very important for a successful marathon experience.

The race itself will be an experience of a lifetime. Most of us have already accepted the fact that, short of a miracle of astronomical proportions, we will not likely win. Despite this there is often an enormous urge for runners to bolt from the start as if there was a herd of wildebeest on a rampage behind them.

Fortunately there are no wildebeest in the Cayman Islands. The common sense advocated by coaches and training programs is to start your run slowly. Runners should conserve their energy for when they'll need it later in the race. If they don't do this they will suffer later and possibly end up walking a sizeable distance at the end. The last few miles may seem like a hundred.

There is a saying that you can divide a marathon into two halves. One half is the first 20 miles. The second half is the last 6. If you conserve your energy the last half will be so much more enjoyable.

Along the run there are 'Stations' at regular intervals that provide water and sports drinks (e.g., Gatorade or Powerade), and some-times food as well, such as orange slices, energy bars or cookies, and bananas among other things. It's vitally important to stay hydrated through the race, especially in hot and humid conditions. Food's that are high energy sources are important also.

Runners may also decide to take their own drinks and/ or food. Some popular energy foods include energy bars, carbohydrate gels like Carb-BOOM and Gu. Clif Shots are another option. These are organic energy chews, some of which may also have caffeine for an extra boost. Runners may bring other foods they like or those that may give them quick sugar-boost.

The run itself is fantastic in many ways. As a runner you put yourself to the test. There is no magic here. You'll either finish or you won't. Along the way you'll meet lots of other runners and may even develop life-long friendships. Your emotions may ebb and flow; there could be euphoric rushes and crushing thoughts that question why you are running and speculate if you will make it to the finish.

But it's highly likely you will, especially if you have dedicated the weeks and months to training. Unless you sustain an injury in the run itself, you will finish for the very reason that you began the training in the first place – the resolve, the tenacity, the patience and determination, and the goal you set for yourself for whatever reason to run the marathon.

The key advice from those who have run over 100 marathons is to enjoy your first ever marathon – be much less concerned about your time and be more focused on enjoying the moment. The first marathon is very special. You can always train for better times in subsequent marathons.

As you run over the finish time the pains and suffering and doubts fade away as the realization sets in that you've done what you set out to do. The proof, asides from the fact that you've stopped running, is that a volunteer or race organizer has just placed a medal on you to recognize and symbolize something very special. Something that only 0.001% of the population has accomplished.

You may finish the race with sore muscles and develop an interesting walk to signal that your body has just made itself move 26.2 miles. You may not have realized it during the race, but your feet may be full of blisters and your toes bruised. Your skin may be chaffed in certain areas if you haven't put some Vaseline on to prevent abrasion.

The stiffness you experience may be alleviated at massage tents which are often provided at the finish lines. The experts, in fact, suggest that a massage between 24-48 hours after a race is highly beneficial for rejuvenating muscles.

Not too long after the race the painful memories quickly fade away. Many runners start planning for their next marathon. Being able to travel to great places makes the experience quite addictive.

Every race is different. There are different locations (urban, rural), different courses (Loops, point to point), different terrain (hills, flat), different runners (old, young, different nationalities), different weather (hot, sun, cold, wind, rain), and different training and experiences.

In the Cayman Islands context, the marathon is a flat looped course that winds its way out of George Town along the coast and back again. It starts in the dark and ends in the sun. Quite unique.

Chapter 4

The Emergence of Marathon Running

At some point while training for your marathon you might wonder how it all got started. Or maybe you won't wonder at all and it will make no difference to how you run. The thing is, the 'marathon' has blossomed from legend to social mainstream. Now, 110 years since the first modern day Olympic marathon, we are witnessing a significant social transformation in marathon running.

The 17 runners in that first Olympic marathon in 1896 would not have imagined there would be 16,000 runners finishing a marathon at a place called Disneyworld, many of whom were taking photos and high-fiving Disney characters along the way. It also required another 3,500 people to volunteer at Disneyworld to make the race happen.

We need to back up. First, the legend ...

The legend is the story of Pheidippides, a runner-messenger (a hemeroromoi – all day-runner), who in 490 BC ran from Marathon to Athens to announce that the 20,000 strong invading Persian army had been miraculously defeated by a significantly smaller Athenian army. This was the Battle of Marathon. The Persians suffered heavily, with 6,400 soldiers killed. The Greeks meanwhile, lost just 192.

Without the help of Aid Stations, porta-potties, a watch, an MP3, Asics running shoes, or gels or gu's, Pheidippides ran as fast as he could to reach Athens and tell the news.

Why? Because the Athenians were prepared to burn Athens to the ground if their army was defeated, which they had all expected. He needed to get there before the bonfire began.

He managed to run the 25 mile distance in time and announced 'We have won'.

Or he may have said 'Rejoice, we have conquered'. No one knows exactly, but these are the most commonly accepted accounts.

The more significant thing perhaps is that he then dropped dead.

Exhaustion.

In 1879 Robert Browning wrote a poem about Pheidippides that reignited interest in running long distances. It's reported that the poem inspired those of sufficient position and importance to make the marathon an official event in the first modern Olympics, held in Athens in 1896.

Most of the 17 runners who started in the first Olympic marathon – from Marathon to Athens – were Greek. At 2pm on April 10, the runners set off from a bridge in Marathon after hearing the Starters speech. They'd been taken to Marathon the night before; some of them had competed in other Olympic events the previous day.

Only 10 finished the race. This officially went to nine when it was discovered the 3rd place runner had cheated. All the runners walked at some point in the race. The winner was Spiridon Louis – who, for 'training', ran alongside the horse-cart his father drove transporting fresh water from the countryside into Athens each day. Overnight he became a national hero. He never competed again.

The 1896 Olympic marathon was an all male affair. Women were not allowed to run in the Olympic marathon until 1984, almost 90 years later. By 2006, there were almost 160,000 women finishing marathons in the United States alone.

The actual length of 'a marathon' was not consistently fixed in the early 1900s. The arbitrary distances of somewhere around 25 and 26 miles were more associated with the local context of the given races. This was also the case for the Olympic marathons.

At the 1908 Olympic Games held in London the marathon distance was meant to be exactly 26 miles. It was to start on 'The Long Walk' in the grounds of Windsor Castle. On the day before the race – to be started by King Edward VII – the distance was extended because it was felt that as the King had a cold, it would be best that he did not go out. Instead, he started the marathon from the Great Courtyard of the Castle (which was 385 yards up the hill).

By doing this the competitors could still finish in front of the Royal Box where his wife – the Queen – would be waiting in the Olympic Arena (White City Stadium). Thus the distance was 26 miles 385 yards (42.195 km).

In the 1912 Olympics the length was changed to 25 miles (40.2 km) and in the 1920 Olympics it was 26.56 miles (42.75 km). Finally, in 1921 the International Amateur Athletic Federation (IAAF) adopted the now official distance – that which the runners raced when the King told them to get going in 1908.

In the early 1900s, the marathon, as Switzer and Robinson note, 'exemplified endurance, energy, exhaustion and heroism'. Many new marathons emerged around the world. But there were also growing concerns that running a marathon would be bad for you – it had a sense of danger about it because it was pushing the limits of what was possible for the human body. Its mystique was also enlarged by the fact that few runners, only those with toughness and stamina, actually took on the distance. These folks were physically gifted it seemed. It wasn't until the 1970s that it was 'discovered' that the distance was also quite possible for non-elite performers.

There was a boom in marathon running. It may partly be explained by the emergence of big city marathons in the 1970s and early 1980s, including London, New York and Berlin. With these events being televised it was clear to thousands of viewers that the distance was possible for many.

In his book The Lore of Running, Tim Noakes comments that there was an exponential growth of marathon running between 1976 and 1980. He adds that while there were just 120 runners in the New York marathon in 1970, this had increased to 2,002 in 1976, and then to 16,315 in 1984. By the year 2000, there were almost 30,000 competing.

Similarly, the first London marathon had just over 6,000 runners in 1981, but by 2001 the number had grown to over 30,000. The popularity of these two races is so high now that lotteries are held each year to see of those who register who will be lucky enough to have their name drawn and be able to run.

We are now witnessing a new boom in marathon running. The appeal is much less to do with running faster and faster times. There is more interest in the social aspect of running, attainment of personal goals, running for charities, the satisfaction of finishing, and enjoying the experience.

In the past few years the increase in the number of people running marathons has been striking. A report by MarathonGuide.com notes that while 299,000 runners finished marathons in the United States in 2000, the number had increased to 397,000 in 2006. Almost 40% of all runners are women. Over 350 marathons were run in the US alone in 2006.

The average age of marathon runners in the United States is almost 40. The largest single age group for males is the 40-44 group (16% of all men), while for women it is the 25-29 age group (18% of all females).

There were 7,025 sub 3-hour finishers (10.7% of all finishers) in the United States in 2006. These are fast times for sure. But the majority of marathon runners are running much slower than this.

My own data from Canada, tell a similar story. Based on data from 82% of all finishers in Canada in 2006 (18,405 of 22,558 finishers from the 21 major races in Canada), 38.1% are women (7,013 women). The largest single age group for males is the 40-49 group (35% of all men), although for women it is the 30-39 age group (34.2% of all females), with the 40-49 age group represented by 31.2% of all females.

The winning time for the very first Olympic race in 1896 (about 25 miles) was 2:58:50. The World Record for the longer and now accepted marathon distance of 26.2 miles today is just over 2 hours at 2:04:55. Paul Tergat of Kenya broke Khalid Kannouchi's world record by 38 seconds at the 2003 Berlin Marathon, and by so doing became the first runner to finish a marathon in under 2:05:00.

The women's world record is held by Paula Radcliffe from Great Britain, who ran a time of 2:15:25 in the London Marathon in April

2003. She broke her own previous world record by almost two minutes.

The half-marathon distance is also increasing in popularity. And the runners are fast in this event also. In the time it takes to watch an episode of CSI, you can run the half marathon distance of 13.1 miles. If that is, you happen to be the male world record holder – Samuel Wanjiru of Kenya – who ran the half marathon in 58:35, on March 17, 2007, in The Hague, The Netherlands. Not far behind Samuel is the women's world record holder – Elana Meyer of South Africa – who ran the distance in a time of 1:06:44 in January 1999, in Tokyo, Japan.

Most half-marathon runners are nowhere near these times. In fact, most finish in times of 2 hours or more. It is a great distance to run, and some runners much prefer to run this distance than the full marathon. It's also a great way to build up for a full marathon.

Chapter 5

The Cayman Islands

Although it's hard to imagine people not living on the Cayman Islands there is no evidence of any existence prior to Christopher Columbus in 1503. In search for the first destination marathon, or possibly a route to the Far East, he instead saw turtles swimming around the islands. The islands were initially named the Las Tortugas, after the sea turtles, one of whom is the logo of the Cayman Islands marathon.

There were three islands spotted by Columbus – Grand Cayman, Little Cayman and Cayman Brac. Not surprisingly there are still three islands, although it is on Grand Cayman where most Caymanians live and where the Cruise ships and other tourists come to visit, including marathoners from all over.

Word got out that the Cayman Islands actually existed and in 1586 Francis Drake arrived. By this time the islands were known as the Caymanas – the Carib word for marine crocodiles (likely the lizards on the islands). There are no crocodiles on the islands now. No-one lived permanently on the islands but they were a popular destination for weary pirates looking for a break, and folks with an appetite for sea turtles. Even then there was a holiday spirit.

Drake reported that you could eat the crocodiles; an important fact for sailors out at sea for lengthy periods. But it was the turtle that was more in demand as ships looked for fresh meat for the crews. Bad news for the turtles.

The first known permanent settlers were two deserters from the British Army who arrived in the 1660s from Jamaica, just 180 miles away. The first recorded permanent inhabitant was Isaac Bodden, born on the islands in 1700. Isaac was the grandson of one of the original settlers.

Perhaps in pursuit of the deserters or simply realizing it was a good idea to own and occupy another tropical paradise, the British Government seized the opportunity, and formally said the islands were possessions of the Royal Crown in 1670. The islands were administered from Jamaica, where the British were already busy creating the foundations for one of the top cricket teams in the world.

Meanwhile, the Cayman Islands continued to be cricket-free, and a safe haven for holidaying pirates and anyone else looking for sun, sand, sea, a good time and plenty of turtles. It was Blackbeard, in fact, who, by now bored with cricket, organized the first marathon in the area as a way of competing with fellow pirates to see who had the ship with the most athletic prowess and endurance.

No he didn't. But it would've have made a great story.

Today you can still see the sun, sand, sea and turtles, but Blackbeard and the other pirates have long gone. Or their hideaways much more sophisticated.

These days you can get your share of pirates, parrots, rum, skulls, treasure and plundering in the Pirates Festival Week held each year in the Cayman Islands. It's a 30-year old tradition – a week of costume competitions, parties, street dances, 5km and 10 km runs, swimming competitions, parades, a Landing Pageant and many children's activities. There is something for everyone.

By the 1730s, despite attacks from hungry Spanish privateers, permanent British settlements had begun on the islands. Over the next hundred years or so the main activities, asides from doing very little at all, were cotton farming, turtle hunting, and salvaging ships that had gone aground around the islands (an activity known as 'wrecking'). There is the famous story of the 'Wreck of the Ten Sails' when a ship hit a reef and was then run into by nine other ships that were following. Because the Cayman community rallied to help the vessels King George III granted the islands tax-free status. The Cayman Islands is now the fifth largest financial center in the world, which goes to show that a bit of human compassion and community support can go a long way.

By the 1800s there were still less than 1,000 people living on the islands. Half of these were slaves, although slavery was abolished in 1835. As the islands moved into the 1900s, cotton exports, fishing and ship building were the main industries.

In 1937 the first Cruise Ship, the Atlantis, visited the Islands. In 1953 the first airfield opened in the Cayman Islands, and tourism had arrived as a viable – very viable – industry. In the same year, Barclay's Bank opened as the first Commercial Bank on the Islands. In 1966 the Islands passed legislation to encourage the banking sector to develop. The islands were becoming a place where both people and money flowed.

By 1970 the population of the Cayman Islands was just over 10,000. Today, about 46,000 people live in the Cayman Islands.

There is no direct taxation which makes the Cayman Islands a major offshore financial center. As of 2003 over 68,000 companies were registered in the Cayman Islands, including almost 500 banks and 800 insurance companies.

In September 2004, the Cayman Islands were hit by Hurricane Ivan. Hurricane Ivan is ranked as the 9th most intense Atlantic hurricane on record. With wind speeds of about 170 miles per hour it caused enormous damage to the Islands as well as loss of life. A quarter of the buildings on the Islands were reported to be uninhabitable. By March 2005, only half of the pre-Ivan hotel rooms were usable. The costs of the destruction totalled over $1.8 billion US dollars. You can still see the damage today, although there has been a huge amount of rebuilding.

Tourism accounts for about 75% of foreign currency earnings. The tourist industry focuses on the luxury market. Over 2.2 million tourists came to the Islands in 2006, half of whom were from the United States. Most of the tourists – 1.9 million in 2006 – come in a Cruise Ship. A big ship I suppose. But they never come on a Sunday as the Islands have maintained that there will be no Cruise Ships in the harbours on a Sunday.

About 90% of the islands' food and consumer goods must be imported, as well as all its fresh water. Those that live on the Islands though, have one of the highest standards of living in the world. There is also plenty to see and do.

That's enough about the Cayman Islands for now. It is a fun, easily accessible, very safe place to visit, with plenty to do. And a great place to live. We'll return there later.

Next up though, the marathon experience.

Facts and Figures

Race History

A tradition starts somewhere. For the Cayman Islands marathon the tradition started in 2002. The event hasn't been going for long but a lot has happened in this short period.

A local woman, Tara Tricket, decided to organize a marathon as a way of raising funds for the Cayman Cadet Corps. In the inaugural event, there were 25 marathoners and 69 half-marathoners running. Including Rhonda Kelly of the Cayman Islands Event company Kelly Holding, who ran in the half-marathon.

It is a huge undertaking to organize an event such as the marathon weekend, especially for one person. Rhonda said to Tara that if she wanted, Rhonda's company would be happy to organize the event. In April 2003 Rhonda got the call. From that point on Kelly Holding has been the event organizer and Rhonda Kelly the Race Director. As Rhonda has commented "We had no idea what we were getting into".

In December 2003 the second marathon weekend took place. Kelly

Holding put its own resources into organizing the weekend and continued to commit the proceeds to the Cayman Islands Cadet Corp. In 2004 they tried to make the event bigger and better. Hurricane Ivan, however, had other plans. Ivan swept through the Caribbean in September of that year. Given the destruction, especially on the south side of the island where the marathon is run, it was decided to postpone the weekend.

So the 2004 marathon weekend was held instead in March 2005, and was one of the first major sporting events on the Islands after Ivan. In the 2005 year, 102 runners finished the half marathon and another 15 finished the full marathon. Eighteen teams competed in the marathon relay. Most of the runners were living in the Cayman Islands.

Given the March event it was decided not to run the marathon weekend in November 2005. And so the 2006 Marathon weekend was the fourth time the event had been held.

In the intervening months Kelly Holding actively sought sponsorship and developed promotional material for the 2006 weekend.

Brochures were distributed on the Islands and at the 2006 Boston marathon. AllSports Central, the American-based timing company that works with Kelly Holding on the logistics of the races leading up to and during the Cayman Islands weekend (especially registration and race timing), also promoted the event on its website. As a result of the promotions, five times as many foreign runners competed in 2006.

Why hold the event in early December? Despite what the runners may think, especially when the sun comes out, it is typically one of the mildest weekends in the year. It's also a shoulder season for tourism when the numbers of tourists are lower than peak season, and the cost of hotel accommodation considerably less as a result.

For those in Canada and the northern American states, early December also means the early part of winter. If there hasn't already been a snow storm, it's probably not far away. In 2006 several runners were escaping the snow and others just avoided snow storms as they travelled to the Cayman Islands to run. A weekend in the tropics is quite appealing when compared to grey skies, snow, cold temperatures and leafless trees.

In the words of Rhonda Kelly, when Kelly Holding committed to organizing the marathon, it "knew nothing about how to go about organizing one". But with each year Kelly Holding has sought to improve the event. The 2003 winner – Tony Keely – said afterwards that he felt it was great race. It was a great compliment. It inspired Kelly Holding to learn more from the runners in order to continually improve the event. Kelly Holding asks everyone what they liked and what they didn't like about the weekend. It's important that people have a great experience. If there is just one bad experience the word gets out. This is especially so in a small Island community.

Since 2003 the number of finishers in the full marathon has increased from 17 to 48 in 2006. The number of half marathon finishers has increased from 62 to 224. As Rhonda says, "It's exhilarating to see how much its grown".

The Course

The full Marathon course is a flat and fast two Loop course (the half-marathon is a one-loop run). The race route is IAAF-sanctioned. The race begins at Breezes by the Bay at the waterside in George Town. Participants run along the waterfront on the South Side of the island. It may be dark when the race begins at 5am but it is certainly not cold. Start-line temperatures are typically in the low 70s (20-22 degrees Celsius). By the end of the marathon the temperature has casually wandered into the higher 70's (24 C). There is a festive air about everything at the start line. It's great to run as a tropical day unfolds in front of you.

Most of the race is along the South Sound out to John Bodden Bay and back. If you run the full marathon you run 4 times around Crawl Bay while trying not to think of its name. You also try to forget at various times that you are running past "Pull and be Damned Point" – an ominous spot for anyone thinking about these sorts of things. If you're still into contemplation and looking for 'signs', you are presented with the "Garden of Reflection" at the turnaround point in the Loop.

You can run away from any negative reflections as you pass through the abundant water stations, placed at every mile along the course. It should come as no surprise that there is water available at each of these. Sports Drinks are also provided at every water station, as well as music and various forms of water station entertainment. The music can be anything really; Caribbean flava, steel pan music, rock, disco, swing, air band ... even country.

"I **enjoyed** the run, the scenery and the **island**. The water stations were great, so **MOTIVATIONAL**, inspiring. They encouraged me to continue when I felt like stopping." (Julie Stackhouse)

The Cayman Islands Marathon 2006 Course Map

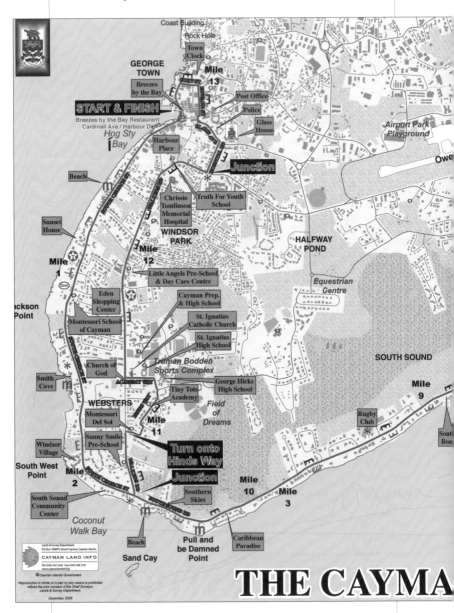

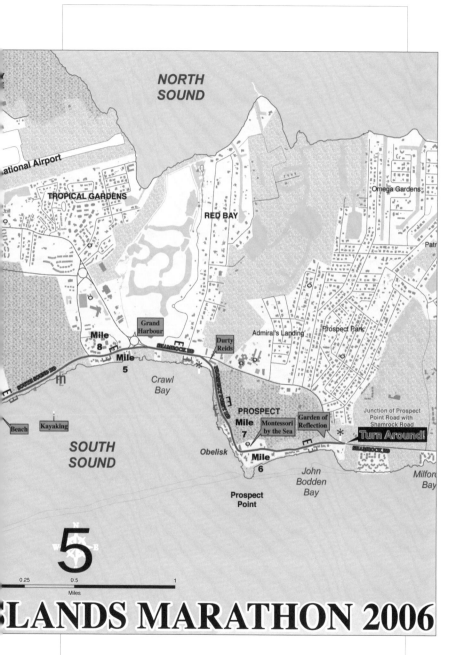

SLANDS MARATHON 2006

First Aid Stations are located every 2 miles on the course and medic stations are at the start/finish line and at the 7 and 20 Mile marker. Medical personnel are also available at several of the stations, start line, and finish area. Members of the Cayman Islands National Red Cross volunteer their time to ensure the safety and first aid care of runners.

The Volunteers

Around two hundred volunteers are required for various jobs like working at Packet Pickup, as road marshals, at the water stations, or doing many other necessary tasks required for ensuring safety and efficiency.

And helping to make it a fun and enjoyable race. After all, if it's not enjoyable, what's the point?

All the volunteers are given special T-shirts and provided with food and drinks the morning of the race.

In 2003 the Event introduced the Water Station competition. Runners vote for the best water station along the course. These volunteer water stations are integral to the course. When you run 13 1/2 or 26 miles, the stations help to mix it up for you – they add variety and fun to the run, not to mention the ability to replenish with water and other liquids. The volunteers at the water stations dress up and entertain enthusiastically – doing whatever they can without inciting riots to support the runners as they pass by. 'The Mexicans' had won the Water Station competition each year leading up to the 2006 Event. As someone said before the 2006 run; "How are you going to beat those Mexicans?"

A month or so after the marathon the organizers host a Thank-You

Appreciation party for the volunteers. Asides from recognizing their essential role in the experience, a draw is held for a return ticket to any Cayman Airways destination.

When asked about their involvement in the marathon weekend, the

"Having never been involved in an event with such broad, international exposure, it was amazing and exciting to be behind the scenes working with other volunteers to make the event run smoothly."

"I volunteered for the marathon because it was a huge event for the Cayman Islands and being a part of something like that, as a Caymanian, is important to me."

"Yes, it is an early time for a start. However, once you arrive and feel the energy throughout one forgets what time it is. It is an Exhilarating Atmosphere from beginning to end! I'm glad that I could be a part of what I felt was a very successful event. Comments from Runners and other attendees were positive and overall the athletes were very impressed. Our Office had a relay team and the challenge has now been placed in our office for the 2007 marathon for the guys to have a relay team and also a few looking at running the 1/2 Marathon. Thanks again and I look forward to helping next year."

"I arrived on the Island in January 2006 on work and was very much interested in running the half marathon in December 06 with two of my friends. Unfortunately my friends had to leave the Island before December 06 on unforeseeable personal grounds. Therefore I could not train as necessary and build up my stamina on my own. But since this was my first year, I was determined to be a part of the Cayman Marathon and to catch the fun. In the meantime an advertisement caught my eye which said "if you are not running the Marathon, then come help us as a volunteer". Hence I decided to be a volunteer! I was helping out at the finish line with the medals and hope to run the 2007 half marathon this year!

Volunteering
"I'll be back again"

My home was trashed during Ivan, and as I no longer have the space to host my children, we see each other less frequently. Thus, when my daughter wrote she was training for the Cayman Islands Marathon as a convenient excuse to come down to visit, I wanted to whole heartedly support her. ... I wanted to cheer her through the rough spots and be there as she crossed the finish line completing her first marathon. Alas, she changed jobs and cities shortly before the marathon and vacation planning took a back seat. She does continue to train, continues to eat healthy, and continues to improve her life style. There I was, I had already volunteered, I already knew Rhonda and the team at Kelly Holding. I could easily meet my commitment. And what a pleasure to do so. My initial job was to deliver breakfast to the supporting police officers and all the water stops. As such, I was the first person to greet the water stop volunteers and got a good sense of conditions out there which I was able to subsequently report to Rhonda (important as all the radios failed and there was no easy communication between water stops and command central). Once breakfast was delivered and I was able to get my vehicle off the course, I switched to direction giver to the runners as the half marathoners completed their course and the full marathoners and teams continued onward. I was able to witness the initial finishers in all categories. Actually a very thrilling experience; next year, I'll be back again and giving Rhonda's team even more of my time, because the reward to me is truly much more than the effort expended.

The Go Go Girls

I was part of a volunteer group called "Campbells Go Go Girls" giving out water, Gatorade, snacks, muscle gell and yelling "We've got water, we've got Gatorade" and encouraging remarks like "Looking good, you can do it", etc. I volunteered as 25 years ago I ran in two marathons in Miami. It was a wonderful experience and I still remember two old ladies who called out "Looking good, Linda, you can do it!" as I passed. I thought: "How on earth do they know my name?" Apparently these two ladies used binoculars to get the number of the runner, look it up on the sheet and then call out the runner's name. Now that is really entering into the spirit of the race. I also volunteered as I thought it would be fun to get a group from our office, a law firm called Campbells, to dress up, have a theme and music, and try to win the prize of five Cayman Airways tickets, as well as helping the runners and having fun. We spent US$100 on balloons, coloured wigs, outfits, blow-up guitars and microphones, music CDs, table cloths, etc. At 4am we set up our stand on South Church Street. We enthusiastically called out to the runners to encourage them on their way. It was a super event. I felt proud to be part of it, especially as Cayman is my Island and we had many runners from overseas. (I have lived in Cayman for 30 years).

As a first-time volunteer, I was unaware of what to expect; I just knew that it would be a busy morning! Immediately on arrival at the Runner's Information Station, I was inspired by the energy and excitement of the day – well before the sun came up. I got chills at the start when the horn blew and it was that same kind of high energy atmosphere throughout the morning, way after the last runner crossed the finish line. Getting information fed back to us during the race as to the whereabouts of the runners kept the start/finish area in the know and the momentum high as we cheered on the runners from 'base'. Non- stop music and commentary on the event by Vanessa and James..... was fantastically done.

"The memory that sticks out most in my mind is seeing a very tired runner cross the line and immediately say "where do I vote for those hysterical Mexicans and their water stop" ... before he even got his medal, water or congratulatory pats on the back."

"If I don't volunteer to assist with the Runner's Information Booth in December 2007, it will only be because I will be in the marathon itself!"

And "Those Mexicans"...

For the past three years we have participated in the Annual Cayman Islands Marathon, the most recent event being this year in 2006. It has always been a wonderful and emotionally rewarding experience. During this time we have been able to provide much energy and enthusiasm for the participants.

Our water stop is different from most others because we not only give out water; we also try to share our culture, warmth, cheer and soul, a notable characteristic of the Mexican people. After the race, all of the runners have to vote for the best stand, and thanks to them we have won the first prize three years in a row. We believe that the key ingredient is that each one of us puts in our best efforts in order to make the event a success, much like the attitude of the runners participating in the event.

We plan each detail months in advance of the race and believe our Mexican creativity, good communication and team work has made us winners one more time. When our team meets to plan our effort, we conclude with a vision: arriving first at the finishing line! We have learned new things every year, and we have certainly gained experience in how to deal with the mechanics of the race, but most important, we have learned how to keep a high spirit within our team in order to encourage the runners to keep their motivation levels up, and in so doing, finish the race.

Gina Connolly (The Mexicans)

By publishing what Gina just wrote, some secrets of The Mexican's success have been revealed. What you see is the spirit. Yes it is about running the distance and accomplishing the goals you try to achieve. But it is also about experience. Although it's certainly a runner's experience, it's also the volunteer's role that contributes to that experience, and the volunteer's own experiences that make the event quite magical.

The Runners

As much as a marathon weekend doesn't happen without volunteers, it certainly doesn't happen without runners. Despite being a lot easier to organize, and with fewer water stations, it would be an odd event without runners.

The 2006 runners came from all over, were all shapes and sizes and all ages. The tables below describe the 2006 Cayman Island marathoners.

The first thing you notice is that even for a comparatively small marathon weekend there are a lot of runners. While some marathoners love the excitement and buzz of a population the size of a small city running a marathon (e.g., the 15,000-30,000 people running New York, London, Boston or Disney), many people prefer the smaller, more intimate runs.

There's lots of reasons for liking both of course, but when you couple the smaller marathons with an attractive destination devoid of widespread urbanity, skyscrapers, fireworks and massive expos, it's no wonder the smaller events draw people from around the world.

In the half-marathon, 50% of the Cayman Islands marathoners were in the 30-39 age category, with the next highest categories being age 20-29 with 21% and age 40-49 with 17%. There were 24 runners aged 50 or over in the half marathon, with eight of these age 60 or over. One runner was under 20. Fifty-six percent of half marathon runners were women.

As with the half marathon, the largest age category represented in the full marathon was the 30-39 age group, with 42% of all the marathon runners. Thirty-three percent of the runners were women. There was a relatively even spread of age representation for women across the 16 runners. Fifty percent of all men in the full marathon were age 30-39, with the next highest age categories being age 20-29 and 40-49, with 22% each. Four runners (2 men and 2 women) were age 50 or over.

Cayman Islands 2006 Half-Marathon Finishers

Age Group	Female %	Male %	Total %
Less than 20	<1% (1)	0	<1% (1)
20-29	25% (29)	15% (15)	21% (44)
30-39	52% (61)	47% (46)	50% (107)
40-49	15% (18)	20% (19)	17% (37)
50-59	3% (4)	12% (12)	7% (16)
60-69	3% (3)	5% (5)	4% (8)
70+	0	0	0
Not Stated	<1% (1)	0	<1% (1)
% and Total # of Finishers	100 (#=117)	100 (#=97)	100 (#=214)
Note: Percent may not equal 100% as numbers rounded			

Cayman Islands 2006 Marathon Finishers

Age Group	Female %	Male %	Total %
Less than 20	0	0	0
20-29	25% (4)	22% (7)	23%(11)
30-39	25% (4)	50% (16)	42%(20)
40-49	38% (6)	22% (7)	27%(13)
50-59	12% (2)	6% (2)	8%(4)
60-69	0	0	0
70+	0	0	0
% and Total # of Finishers	100% (#=16)	100% (#=32)	100% (#=48)
Note: Percent may not equal 100% as numbers rounded			

And so the volunteers commit their time and enthusiasm and the organizers resign themselves to 48-hours with little or no sleep. The sleep they may get will involve much tossing and turning thinking about the things still to do and everything that could possibly go wrong.

Runners meanwhile, descend on George Town from all over, bringing their own concerns known only to themselves, and to whoever seems to be interested enough to listen. Not a Pirate or Cruise Ship to be seen.

A lot happens in a short amount of time. Although the final countdown begins with Registration, much has already unfolded behind the scenes as the organizers gear up for the weekend. In many ways, comparatively speaking, the runners have it easy!

"Running helps me clear my mind. Each footstep allows one more problem to fall away." • "The atmosphere of camaraderie and the festive mood which was taken to the volunteerism and other participation was very evident." •

"It was a very wonderful marathon." • The build up to the race is a unique feeling and something we will never forget." • **"The race course was simply outstanding. It was a runner's dream."** • "…the course support was beyond outstanding." •

"You have inspired me to become more or a runner and less of a walker!" • "Running has made me stronger, more confident, and has proven that I have within me the dedication and commitment to accomplish any goal or challenge that stands before me." • **"The intimacy of the race may be one of the best aspects."** • "Our legs were like jelly but we felt amazing and so happy." • *"…the reward to me is truly much more than the effort expended."* • **"I think Cayman is one of the most beautiful places on earth."** • "The satisfaction and sense of accomplishment that running brings is like nothing else." • "It has always been a wonderful and emotionally rewarding experience." • **"The experience will be cherished forever."** • *"…was an achievement I really hadn't imagined I'd complete."* • "During the Marathon I realized how much courage everybody can have in order to succeed." • **"The weather was perfect and it was an amazing experience to start the marathon in a crowd of so many people."** • "I have never felt so good than that day! The Finish was so great." • "The feeling of accomplishment is simply unrivalled by anything I have ever done in my life." • **"…through running I have learnt about myself at the deepest level."** • "It is an Exhilarating Atmosphere from beginning to end!" • *"Running has inspired me to accomplish more than I ever imagined"* • "…a very thrilling experience."

Chapter 7

Gearing Up for the Weekend

The Organizing

Organizing the Cayman Islands marathon begins almost immediately after the previous year's weekend. The organizers meet and discuss what worked and what didn't. A plan is developed that outlines the various dates when things need to happen. Sponsorship is important. Another critical element of early planning is a marketing plan. As there are hundreds of marathons run worldwide each year, the earlier the better it is for promoting the weekend, because many people plan their travel well advance for marathon events.

A month or two before the event things really heat up. Sponsorship details are finalized, and bibs, medals, shirts etc need to be ordered. Timing chips that are to be worn by runners must be assigned to bib numbers. Computer systems need to be synchronised to ensure the timing chips accurately function. Water and sports drinks must be ordered – enough to ensure runners do not go without as has sometimes been the case in other major marathons. Running out of fluids makes some runners cranky to say the least. In the heat of the Cayman Islands, it's absolutely essential that there are plenty of fluids available for the runners.

With just weeks to go staff at Kelly Holding and AllSports Central are fielding all and any questions from interested runners, volunteers, sponsors, and the general public. The media also get involved. It's a major event, especially in the Cayman Islands.

In the week before the race hundreds of details must be taken care of. Like ants in the colony dozens of people play a role, however big or small. Among other things, the course is measured and recertified. Packages – goody bags – are put together for the runners, and registration and timing chip details are worked on.

Two to three days before the weekend the organizers hold a meeting with all the volunteers – outlining the jobs required, and organizing the volunteers into specific roles and functions (e.g., water stations, medical, packet pick-up, finish line, food, etc).

Registration

Registration occurs the day before the run. It takes place at the Marriott Grand Cayman Resort, one of the Sponsors of the Event (located on 7 Mile Beach). There is still a chance for late registrations. At least one competitor first registered to run when she arrived at the airport on Grand Cayman Island. Leaving the airport with her husband she saw the Marathon volunteers greeting race competitors who were arriving for the weekend. Thinking this sounded like a great idea while on vacation she registered on the spot.

While most guests at the Marriott are enjoying their leisurely stay on the beachfront property, perhaps doing plenty of nothing intermingled with not much at all, the runners anxiously arrive to register and set their sights on doing something before doing nothing. And quite the something it is.

At Registration the race bibs are given out. Like the timing chips, which are also provided, these must be worn. Typically they are randomly allocated, although for 2006 the organizers gave Dane Rauschenberg the number 52, because Dane was in the midst of running 52 marathons – one each weekend of 2006 – to raise money for a charity. More on that later.

Not to devalue the interest and importance of the 'bib and chips', the highlight for most runners, apart from meeting up with friends from previous runs, is the Goody Bag. It is like Christmas all over again, but without the wrapping or the turkey. A typical goody bag will include some healthy snacks, possible gifts and a few words from sponsors, things to give your children or grandchildren, information sheets that will likely not be read, and the race T-shirt.

Hopefully the shirt is the size you requested when you first registered for the race, and the colour too, if that's an option.

The Cayman Island shirts for 2006 were a colourful bright yellow or blue, with our buddy the Tortuga looking quite fresh and happy as he runs waving the Cayman Islands flag. Without a trace of sweat noticeable he is clearly in the early stages of the race. Usually you have an option of buying another shirt at a nominal cost as well as receiving one as part of registration. I did.

The Pasta Party

The pasta party was held the night before the race. Most marathons charge a fee to attend the pasta party but for the Cayman Islands marathon it is free. The party is held at Breezes by the Bay. There's great food and a view overlooking the ocean and the intersection immediately below where the race will start and finish. There is an air of excitement and anticipation. There is plenty to talk about. There is plenty of food.

Breezes By The Bay is a picture postcard Tropical Grill and Rhum Deck in the Caribbean. It has magnificent views of Caribbean Sea, from South Sound to Seven Mile Beach, made all the more impressive with two floors of wrap-around balconies. As the brochure notes, "The view, the tropical drinks, the casual, fun approach to waterfront dining "island style" – all of these make Breezes By the Bay the perfect place for breakfast and brunch, lunch and dinner." And a Pasta Party.

In 2006 the sun was shining brilliantly on the Bay as it began its daily setting ritual. The sun, that is. Music played as the tropical breeze blew gently. While there was an option of sitting out on the second storey porch, most people were staying cool, and soaking in the views while they talked inside. Even if you don't know anyone else at the event, by the end of the Pasta Party chances are you will know several runners, and will have shared training, travel and/ or previous race stories. Complete strangers can quickly become life time friends.

As coincidence would have it, in 2006 the last night of the Cayman Islands Jazz Festival began shortly after the Pasta Party. Just a 15-minute walk from Breezes by the Bay, for some runners it was too tempting not to miss an opportunity to see great performers.

Some people may say that it's unwise to go to a Jazz Festival the night before running a marathon. They're probably right. But this is where running intersects with the rest of your life. If it so happens that Natalie Cole, Arturo Tappin, Hi-Tide and Swanky are playing the night before the race, in an outdoor venue on a tropical island and just 10 minutes from your hotel, you are extremely tempted to miss some sleep in exchange for the Jazz experience. You may be quite prepared to lose a few minutes in your race time in exchange for a night of live Jazz music.

Some runners take this Jazz option. Some runners get little sleep before the 5am start. Some runners don't even go to sleep at all and still race the next day. But what a great night of music. Life's trade-offs.

For most runners, it's off to bed for a good night's sleep. The next day they are running either 13.1 or 26.2 miles. Their bodies will appreciate some down time. But some runners may spend a restless night tossing and turning thinking about the next day, even if they do go to bed early.

With a start time of 5am the runners may also be a little concerned about sleeping through the alarm. It's not unusual to wake up several times in the night fearing that you've slept through the alarm. You can see why some people felt it would be easier to stay up, enjoy the Jazz music and not worry about the alarm at all.

I didn't stay up all night but I did go to the festival. I can't say I've ever seen this in the training schedules as a proven strategy for running a marathon, but it was a truly fantastic night; a great experience.

Before the strike of midnight on Saturday night there is still a continuous flow of activities. Importantly, before the course work begins in the early hours of Sunday morning, changes need to be made to the timing chips in response to additions, deletions and modifications to runner's information that had been submitted in the final steps of registration earlier in the day. Some new runners register late, while others decide to run the half-marathon instead of the full marathon.

Why did the runners enter the Cayman Islands marathon?

Runners had many different reasons for running and had many different experiences and training. In their own words, here's what they said.

"It is one of the most BEAUTIFUL places on earth. It also gave me the opportunity to vacation."

Passion and Satisfaction

I started running to get in shape, but I became a "marathoner" because of the passion and love that I developed for running and everything running has given me. There is nothing like getting up before there is anyone on the streets, just my shoes hitting the pavement, with only the night moon and stars in the Cayman sky....to watching the sun rise over the sparkling water in the Sound in my second hour of running....to diving in the refreshing beautiful Caribbean sea of Seven Mile Beach at the end of a long hot 16-miler. The satisfaction and sense of accomplishment that running brings is like nothing else, and living in Grand Cayman, surrounded by its beauty during a run, is almost too breathtaking for words.

Pride

I ran the Cayman Islands half marathon. A friend got me involved in 'preparing' for the marathon approximately six weeks prior to the event. We only had the weekends to practice, but we did our runs Saturdays and Sundays. I DID IT JUST TO SEE WHETHER OR NOT I COULD HAVE. I was never very active all my life, and I viewed it as a challenge at 42 years of age. I did it. I ran 13.2 miles in 2 hours. 45mins. and was very proud of myself. The best part of the whole event was that I enjoyed doing it and plan to continue.

"I had originally planned to run the full marathon but early on I was having a hamstring issue and bailed at the half (well there WAS a finish line after all!). I went on to have a much better day at Houston last weekend (albeit a whole lot cooler)."

A Beautiful Place to Run

I have been to Grand Cayman on several occasions - both business and pleasure. .... I think Cayman is one of the most beautiful places on earth. It is rivalled, in my world traveling experiences, only by the Red Sea. I was 40 years old (now 42) when I ran my first marathon. I am a lawyer and have been a Judge. That type of work is sedentary to say the least and I needed to get in shape. I thought setting a goal to run a marathon would motivate me to get in shape and give me a life-time experience. I ran my first marathon in my home town, the Oklahoma City Memorial Marathon, which helps to benefit survivors of April 19, 1995 tragedy. So it had special meaning to me. I trained hard and finished in 4:48. I found myself "hooked" - it was such an overwhelming feeling of accomplishment! Oklahoma has cold winters and it is easy to get depressed in the cold and early darkness. So I next set my sights on finding a marathon some place sunny in the winter. I ran the Honolulu Marathon in December 2005. It was a GREAT experience. In keeping with the "Island Marathon" theme, I found the Cayman Islands Marathon on-line and simply could not resist going on vacation AND running a marathon.

A Birthday Celebration

I have visited the Cayman islands several times in the past to visit family but this time was more important than ever - I was turning 40 and taking a break from the minus 25 degree Celsius weather back home in Calgary, Alberta Canada. What better way to celebrate my 40th than to run a half marathon.

Travel to the Sun

Our adventure to the Cayman Islands Marathon actually started as somewhat of a joke. Jim, who is almost retired and spends a fair amount of time on the computer, found the marathon while he was surfing the Internet. He sent it to a few running friends and asked "How about this one?", not thinking any of us would be seriously interested. When we weighed the options, a winter weekend in Chicago or a winter weekend in the Cayman Islands, we decided it would be a great idea! We came to the Cayman Islands Marathon as a group from the Chicago area. We all really enjoyed the race. I ran the marathon and was a little worried about doing the loop twice, but since the first time is in the dark, the second time around seems like a whole new race. The race was very well organized and the lack of spectators was more than made up for by the enthusiastic water stations every mile or so. It was a great race.

"Ivan made a mess of our plans to meet in Cayman and run the 2004 half marathon. It is hard to have a race when the road is missing."

"The name "Cayman Islands Marathon" literally leaped off my computer screen. I used to live in Cayman, I love Cayman, I had so many of my life's greatest experiences in Cayman, I met my partner of the last 10 years in Cayman, I could go on and on but I knew I must return and run "down memory lane.""

"My husband was working on the island, I did not know about it. I got off the plane, Jerry [Jerry Harper – Coach of the Cayman Island Phoenix Athletic Club] was sitting there [meeting the marathon runners as they arrived], and I signed up!"

I Wonder if They Have a Marathon There?

I receive confirmation that the Royal Cayman Islands Police have offered me a 2-year contract to work in the Cayman Islands. 'Great' says Colin (my husband) 'I wonder if they have a marathon there?' With that he is surfing the Internet and soon finds the Cayman Islands Marathon web site. He gives me all the information. (Luckily there is a 1/2 marathon option!)

I tell the people at our running club, 'Come and visit at the beginning of December; you can do the marathon!' Several people are interested but for next year they say. But now I feel obliged to run and report back on the course!

Friendships

I chose to run the Cayman Marathon because in August I met David, who lives in Grand Cayman. He was playing tennis tournaments in Europe and spent a week in my town Eastbourne in England. We met because he had arrived and was looking for the tennis courts, so I gave him a lift there. We became friends during the week and then kept in touch when he returned home. I saw there was a marathon on his island – so it was a great opportunity to meet up again and do my sport! He did his sport in my home town and I did my sport on his island!

"My brother is attending Medical School at St. Matthews Medical School on Grand Cayman Island. So I went to see him and got to run a new marathon. And it was also another opportunity to run with Dane Rauschenberg... we overlapped 3 marathons this fall."

Training for the Half Marathon | Part 2

I hate the pressure of races and often end up starting at a faster pace than normal and then not enjoying the run. This time, however, I wanted to run at my own comfortable pace steadily throughout. My training plan for the week leading up to the Half Marathon became totally messed up. I had signed up to play in the Club Championships at the South Sound Squash Club, but as I had not been playing much squash, figured I would get knocked out in the semi-finals on the Wednesday night, run my last training run on Thursday, then be all set for the Sunday morning race. As it turned out I ended up as the #1 seed, had quite a few byes, played on the Monday and Tuesday evenings (after running on those mornings too) and was supposed to play the finals on the Friday night. I managed to convince the organizers to allow the finals to be played on the Thursday night, took the Wednesday as a rest day which meant that the Tuesday was my last run. I then proceeded to win the finals. I was very sore the next day and even sorer on the Saturday from using gluteus muscles that I had not used for 3 weeks. After 8 weeks of training I thought I'd blown it as I was now hurting.

"A friend asked me to run with him. Not to mention it sounded like a great place to visit."

On a Whim

I can't say why, exactly, but I decided to walk the half marathon... I have done a number of 5km and 10km runs in the past, both here in the Cayman Islands and in the Greater Vancouver/Victoria British Columbia area, so this kind of thing wasn't necessarily "new" to me. I heard the ad for the marathon on the radio one day while I was at work, and heard that there was a 1/2 marathon run/walk component, so I decided that that might be fun to give it a try and, on a whim, signed up."

We have **family** in the

Cayman Islands

so this was an OPPORTUNITY to combine a race with a visit.

"[I ran] because I am a Caymanian and it seemed fitting that the first time I attempted this event was at home."

Gearing Up | Part 1

On February 4th 2006 I went for my first one mile run!!! At that time it was hard to imagine running one mile before work but I was determined to lose weight and get fit. I read on the Internet that you need to run for 3 months before you start to see the physical results and also you will then be addicted. It was all true. Slowly but surely my body shape changed and one mile became two and two became three and you know the rest! I bumped into a friend – Ceri – in June, and she commented on how great I looked and I told her it is all the running before work. She asked to join me and I said great – run a mile or two and chat with someone, excellent. We ran for a while and then decided maybe we should enter a race and have a goal to aim for. Perfect. Lets enter the Cayman Islands Half Marathon!!! What a goal! We started our training schedule on July 31st for 18 weeks. Now, if someone had told me I would be running 5 miles before work I would have said "no way". My weight continued to drop and the physical change was amazing and what a feeling let me tell you. I had lost 28 lbs before the race! Ceri and I participated in a few local fun runs before the half marathon and that showed us how we need to start off slow at the beginning and what we need to work on for the "big" race. Our goal for the half marathon was to finish without having to walk and within 3 hours and 15 minutes. The build up to the race is a unique feeling and something we will never forget, the achievement of just finishing the training program and getting a race packet was massive.

Relay Powerhouse

Back in London I used to walk everywhere, but coming to Cayman Islands eliminated that part of my daily workout routine. Looking around the Island I soon realized that there is a huge running community and I decide to take up running to keep stay fit. A friend told me that she was training for the Cayman Islands half marathon and I got interested. Soon after, I had to admit to myself that I wasn't quite fit enough for a half marathon. While looking around for other options I discover that the Cayman Island marathon organizers had a solution to my problem; the 4 Person Relay Team! I just needed a goal to continue running in the tropical heat three times a week, and this was it. At first I tried to persuade my friends to run, but without success. Then I found out that my employer RE/MAX Cayman Islands was one of the main sponsors of the event. I pitched my idea to my boss James Bovell, Owner/Broker at RE/MAX. He suggested that I should ask around the company if three other runners would like to join me. In the end I signed up several agents namely Amanda Brookman, Kerri Kanuga and Kass Coleman who are all RE/MAX agents. Now the next big question was; Who is going run which part of the course? We decided that only a draw out of the hat would be fair. I was the lucky one who started the run at Breezes followed by Amanda then Kerri, and our last runner was Kass. Once that was all sorted we started to look for a suitable name. Team RE/MAX was just too boring, and so we went for RE/MAX Power House, having in mind that we are strong women who enjoy running. On the day itself I had a fantastic time. The weather was perfect and it was an amazing experience to start the marathon in a crowd of so many people. I enjoyed every minute of it and was very pleased with our team performance and my personal time. We didn't quite win the run but still had a great time and encouraged some of our fellow RE/MAX agents to put a team together next year. There is rumor of a 'men only' team who will set out to beat the RE/MAX Power House. Let's see who wins on the 2nd of December 2007!

A month before the race I started to lose interest. A week to go and I seriously thought of not running. But then I thought of all the publicity from last year – my picture on all the promotional material. How many, or who had been inspired by that? I decided it wasn't about last year. It was about this one and so I went for it. I was just about overwhelmed when I crossed the start line – being amongst so many other runners. Yes, so many, compared to previous years. I looked at Rhonda and if I had caught her eye I know I would have definitely broken down. One of these years there will be 500, 1000 and more runners. And guess what? I guh be deh! What about you?

Chapter

Race Day

"It was a very wonderful marathon."

Race Day. Excitement. Anticipation. Nervousness. Adrenalin rush. Energy. Tension. Uncertainty. Non-stop action.

And that's just the organizers.

Race day for the organizers – Kelly Holding, the volunteers and AllSportCentral starts at midnight when the streets on the course can be closed. As Steve Kurtenbach from AllSportCentral observed; "The race starts at 12:01. There's a ton of stuff that has to happen in the five hours before the race starts".

In the early hours the remote equipment is tested out on the course – for example at the furthest point on the course at the 1/4 mark for the marathon (half-way for the half-marathon). At the start/finish line there is a primary system and a separate back-up system set up. And just in case, there are also 3-4 people manually backing up the timing as well to ensure exact times are given as runners cross the line. Anything can happen so back-ups are essential. Someone could always drive over equipment, for example, as in fact happened in this 2006 event.

The Start/Finish line must be set-up, which as the photos show, requires more than a chalk line drawn on the road. The scaffolding and facade must be erected, the timing chip mats are laid down, and tables, tents, balloons, barriers, etc. are all put in place. Out on the course meanwhile, the mile markers must be set-up – and at the right place – which can be quite challenging in the 3am darkness.

Throughout the five-hours of darkness there's a continual influx of people that seemingly drop out of the sky bringing supplies or set-ting-up various parts of the course – including the water stations.

Around 4am the runners themselves start showing-up. There is no one particular instant when everyone arrives, as by this point the runners are all operating on their own schedule that works best for them, or they may have no choice as to when to arrive if they're be-ing transported by others. Those staying at Hotels meanwhile, are offered a pick-up shuttle service which they arrange at registration the day before.

Several hundred runners descend on the start-line in this one-hour period. As the tables indicated the 2006 marathon attracted a re-cord number of competitors: 48 finishers (32 men, 16 women) in the marathon, 214 finishers (97 men, 117 women) in the half marathon, and 31 relay teams. That's a lot of anxious bodies milling around in the dark making their last preparations before they disappear down the road.

As well as the runners there are the supporters – friends and family members – who stay with the runners until the last minute. For those who require it there is a bag-drop-off service available so that runner's belongings can be safely stored. The organizers and volunteers mean-while, field questions continuously while they do the final necessary work to get the race away on time. It may look chaotic, but it works.

Countdown begins. Runners are requested to get behind the start-line. It's well organized and pretty clear that the race will begin right on 5am. You look around as you make final adjustments to laces, glasses, hats, MP3s, clothing, and make final visits to washrooms and so on. Runners smile and laugh. Some are quiet and reserved.

There is the shaking of hands, and in the true spirit of distance running strangers are wishing one another good luck for the race. As is often expressed, everyone is a winner already because of the very fact that they are present to start the run. As John Bingham states "The miracle isn't that I finished. The miracle is that I had the courage to start".

The gun goes off and we cross the Start line with the sound of the timing chip registering as we go over the line. There is cheering all around.

And so in the darkness of 5am Sunday morning, all the runners take off together from in front of Breezes by the Bay Restaurant to run the full or half marathons, or to run as part of the relay teams. It is a wonderful moment. Everyone shares the same experience but it resonates in different ways.

Within a few minutes the festive noise and excitement is replaced by the sound of running shoes hitting the ground and runners talking to one another. Some runners have already turned on their MP3 players and will use their selected sounds as comforts and inspiration along the run.

The serious competitors that could actually place have long left the bulk of the runners. We'll see them, albeit briefly, as they fly by us on the return portion of their run.

The Half-Marathon

First to finish are the half-marathon runners. Some finish in the dark – quick enough to avoid the rising sun. Four runners finish before 6:30am. Another 55 runners finish in under 2 hours, before the sun really starts to hit the day. Most, however, come over the line in the next two hours; 129 runners finish between 2 and 3 hours, and 26 runners finishing between 3 and 4 hours 10 minutes.

Marius Acker, who lives in the Cayman Islands, is the first to finish the half-marathon, with a time of 1:19:49. In very close second place was Marco Napierala with 1:20:01, with another Cayman Island resident Dave Walker third in 1:25:22.

In the women's half-marathon event Maria Mays, who also lives in the Cayman Islands was first, with a time of 1:26:58. Second place was Katrina Rowe with a time of 1:41:47, while Marion Pandohie finished third with a time of 1:43:25.

With the exception of Marco Napierala from Europe, the top 10 finishers in the half-marathon are all currently living in the Cayman Islands.

Maria Mays | 1st Women's Half Marathon

Maria comes from England and has been living in the Cayman Islands for the past 3 1⁄2 years. She says because the Cayman Islands is a very outdoorsy place it's easy to be fit and healthy. "It has a massive running community. People run constantly". She runs to and from work every day for a total daily distance of about 10 miles. Local residents have come to get used to her running. A complete stranger recently stopped Maria in the Supermarket and asked 'what shall I be doing with my hands when I'm running'.

Maria ran several half-marathons in 2006, mostly in the United States. She looked at where there were direct flights from the Islands to the US to ease the travel. Maria typically runs in the smaller half-marathons (less than 300 people). As she notes "it's a great way to see a country and to meet people".

When she was growing up Maria said she was "rubbish at ball sports", so she did cross-country running instead. The marathon distance, she feels, is a punishing distance whereas half-marathons seem like a perfect distance. Maria also does triathlons. She's not keen on the swimming but loves the running and cycling. But she says that running can be much more social than swimming or cycling because you can talk with others while running – hard to do when you're cycling. Even harder when you're swimming.

Thoughts on the race: Maria says it's a friendly course. This was her second time running in the half-marathon. "It's a pretty course once it gets light". And for such a small place it's a "fantastic event". When asked about how she paces herself in a race Maria says she only has one speed and so the half marathon distance seems ideal. For the Cayman Islands half-marathon she was hoping to beat a time of 1:25. But she actually had the flu during the race. While everyone else was thinking about the heat and humidity Maria was freezing cold from the Start to the Finish Line.

Maria's advice for people interested in running: Start off by mixing walking with running and then gradually increase the distance with the walk, run, walk, run approach. "The great thing about running is that all you need is a good pair of running shoes and that's it." The only other costs are over to you. There is no 'right' or 'wrong' about running. Asides from getting or keeping in shape, and losing or maintaining weight, you're able to get out and see places. It's especially great when you travel to other places because you get to see so much more.

Marius Acker | 1st in the Men's Half Marathon

Marius is a South African who has lived on the Cayman Islands for 1 1⁄2 years. He is 35 years old, and works in an Investment company in the Cayman Islands. He competes in triathlons and is an avid surfer. "When there's surf I don't train", he says. He has run marathons in South Africa, New Zealand and the United States (Boston), and looking at possibly running in the Chicago marathon in 2007. His aim is to run a marathon every year, although he focuses his training more on triathlons and the smaller distances such as the half-marathon and 10 km runs.

Thoughts on the race: Marius was running with a hamstring injury he had aggravated a week earlier in a triathlon event in the Cayman Islands. He didn't run at all in the week leading up to the half-marathon. During the race itself his aim was to control his run and see how he felt in the later stages. It was a closely fought men's half-marathon, with second place Marco Napierala from Germany finishing just a few seconds after Marius. With just over a mile left Marcus started sprinting and was able to establish a lead that he maintained till the finish. The Water Stations, he said "were out of this world". Third was Marcus' training friend Dave Walker.

Running in the Cayman Islands: In a typical week Marius will train in the morning between 7am and 8am, and then sometimes in the afternoon as well. In the weekends he runs along 7-Mile Beach. There are virtually no hills on the Islands – which makes it challenging if you want to do any hill training. Marius says that if you're not a sporting or outdoors person, you might get bored in the Cayman Islands. He said that two months prior to the marathon weekend "people were running like crazy", training for their races. It's best to train early in the morning before the sun comes out or later when the sun is going down. Humidity can be a problem so it pays to drink plenty of fluids. If you are thinking of running the full marathon he says, you need to get used to running in the heat and humidity.

Marius said it would be okay for the Chicago folks to come to the Cayman Islands again and run in the full marathon this coming year, as he'd like to win the half marathon again in 2007.

The Relay

In the Relay marathon event it was the 'Hy-Tech Tigers' made up of national team runners that took top honours, winning in a time of 3:05:18. Second place went to 'Revolution' with a time of 3:22:23, with third going to 'Monograms & More Daily Grind' in a time of 3:27:28.

The top ten relay teams finished the marathon in under four hours. The remaining 21 teams all finished in less than 5:02 hours. Of the 31 Relay teams just two were from off the islands; The Four Horsemen from Canada (8th), and The Connecticut Colonials from the US (17th). There were some other great team names and shirts, including The Rumrunners, Suckers for Punishment, KISS and Run, The Hopefuls, and Last Minute Layabouts.

The Marathon

The results for the full marathon were notable in several ways. The overall winner was Julie Stackhouse (age 27) of Florida – who was running her first ever marathon! Julie is the first woman to win the Cayman Islands Marathon. Her time of 3:06:17 also set a new course record for women.

With the different types of runners (half and full marathoners and the various relay teams), Julie said that it wasn't until about Mile 14 that she had a sense of where she was in the race.

She said afterwards "I can't believe I won. My win is just starting to sink in. I hope to be back next year to defend my title."

In second place was Mark Hydes, age 40, who, as reports on the race observed, "is fast earning the title as the King of the Cayman Islands

Marathon". Mark has now finished second on three occasions. His second place time this year was 3:09:26.

For the first 23 miles Mark and Julie were running close together. Julie later said she was grateful for being able to have the pace together like this for that long a time. Mark said after the race that the last few miles were a struggle. He explained "Julie and I were neck and neck. We were feeding off each other's energy but my legs began to cramp. Keeping hydrated is a fine balance. If you don't drink enough, you get cramps. If you drink too much, you get sick to your stomach."

And so after pushing the pace for 23 miles Mark got cramps, which slowed his efforts and enabled Julie to push ahead of him and maintain her lead over the remaining 3 miles to win the race.

Third place overall in the marathon was Mike Ridsdale. Mike and Julie had been running together earlier in the race. And for a period all three – Mike, Julie and Mark, were running together around the halfway stage (at 1 hour: 33 minutes). But as the race progressed Mike could feel his legs starting to go and Mark and Julie were able to break away.

In all, 48 runners finished the full marathon. The top eight runners finished in less than 3 1/2 hours. The next 12 finished in under 4 hours. The next eighteen runners finished in under 5 hours, and the remaining finishers completed the marathon in 6:02 hours or less. Regardless of where you placed, or what time you finished in, it was a significant achievement.

Julie Stackhouse | Overall Winner of the Marathon

Julie is an Assistant Track coach for the women's team at the University of North Florida in Jacksonville, where she also does personal training. Although she had run in several half marathons before the Cayman event she had never run them competitively. Her competitive track background has been mainly sprinting and the heptathlon. Julie's longest training run leading up to the marathon was two hours.

Julie decided to run in the Cayman Islands marathon after hearing about it from a woman she personally trained for the 2005 race. Julie said "I set a goal, the 2006 Cayman Islands Marathon, started training and I did it." She added; "The victory was surreal. I can't believe the sense of accomplishment. I am hooked on marathons. I can't believe I was first overall."

This first marathon, Julie said, was a combination of experiences – the friendly people, the organization, water stations, scenery – and the overall atmosphere. She was delighted with the run – knowing she had the speed but not so sure whether she had the endurance. That definitely seemed to work though, and now she is looking at more endurance events in the future. "It's addictive", she said.

With the 3:06 time in this first marathon, Julie qualified to race in the Boston marathon, which she ran in early 2007. She'd like to break the 3:00 time in future marathons. Also in Julie's sights are Ironman events.

Mark Hyde | 2nd Overall | 1st Place Men

The marathon event is very much a family affair for Mark. Last year, his sister Gerry Robinson, ran her very first marathon. In 2006 Gerry and another brother, Tim Hydes, ran in the half marathon. Their sister Juana meanwhile, looked after the hydration needs of the family.

Mark didn't start to run until he was 24 years old, and even then it was just to get fit and not necessarily to compete. He set a goal of finishing in the top 10 of his first event – the Compass Fun Run. He finished 10th, and got the running bug. As he said in a race report "I love to compete. The training helps to prepare you, to toughen you up mentally. Running helps me clear my mind. Each footstep allows one more problem to fall away, and when I finish I have a great feeling." Mark says his running is inspired by local Cayman Island runners Malcolm Davis and Roger Davies.

Over the last 15 years Mark has established an international reputation. He has competed in the Caribbean Cross-Country Championship three times, the Island Games, the World Half Marathon and the 24-Hour Relay Race. His favourite race though is the Cayman Islands Marathon. It's also the only marathon he's ever competed in.

He says "I competed in the first Cayman Islands Marathon because it was home. I run in it every year because I want to inspire more people to run. The event is well organised and is growing every year. It is truly an international event."

Rhonda Kelly, the Race Organiser, was quoted soon after the 2006 race as saying "Mark is a fixture at the Cayman Islands Marathon, and we look forward every year to seeing him run...Every year he waits until the very last minute to register which always causes a bit of anxiety as to whether he's actually going to participate, but in the end he is always there on race day not only to support us, but to also make Cayman proud. It's because of people like Mark Hydes that we do this event. He is an inspiration and embodies the spirit of a true sportsman."

Mike Ridsdale | 3rd Overall | 2nd Place Men

Mike is originally from the United Kingdom but has been living in the Cayman Islands for several years. He is the Office Manager for a Cayman Islands Plumbing Company. Mike says he loves getting fit and being fit. He says he "likes to run and just switch off". So he doesn't wear an I-Pod or anything like that. Fortunately he doesn't mind training in the heat.

He trains and competes in triathlons as well as marathons. He also ran in the Chicago marathon. Mike's training for Chicago included long runs that increased in distance over time – up to 20 to 24 miles with shorter runs in between, although he says if he was to do it again he would decrease the longer distances.Despite freezing cold conditions at the beginning, he finished in a time of 3:08 – fast enough to qualify for the Boston marathon.

Mike takes every Monday off – no training at all, which he notes is important for preventing injuries. "You need to take it easy – your body tells you." Unfortunately, in between the Chicago and the Cayman Islands marathons he sustained a hamstring injury.

He was really pleased with the Cayman Islands race this year. He said that in the heat the big guys need to make sure they get enough fluids – this, as other runners commented, was really well done in the Caymans Island marathon. He also ran with his own Gu – which is something for runners of all types to consider, as gels and food can make a big difference to energy levels in a marathon, especially in the heat.

Mike's advice to potential runners in the 2007 Cayman Islands marathon is to not underestimate the weather – especially the humidity. Come prepared, and if possible come a few days earlier to acclimatise. There's plenty to see and do as well.

In 5th place overall and third place for the men was Dane Rauschenberg. Dane had entered the race as part of his one year quest to run

52 marathons in 52 weeks. The Cayman Islands marathon was his 48th of the year.

48th!

While still doing a full-time job in the United States Dane's entire 2006 year – the weekends especially – was dedicated to raising money for the Mobile Alabama Chapter of L'Arche International – a federation of communities where people with a mental handicap share their lives with those that can help. Dane went on to complete his goal of running 52 marathons in 2006. And he's still running and raising money.

On his website www.fiddy2.org Dane described the Cayman Islands marathon. In the following caption, here's some of what Dane wrote:

Dane's Cayman Islands Marathon Recap | Excerpts

On the day before the race, I decided to lay low and soak in some sun in an attempt to wind myself down for an early bedtime. With the 5 AM starting time for the marathon, I knew in order to get a full night's sleep I would have to attempt to be sleeping by 8 PM. Luckily for me, hopping into bed at such an early hour was assisted by an absolutely fabulous pasta dinner, which was included as part of your race registration fee. There are few races where the pasta dinner is included for free and little touches like this do not go unnoticed by the competitors.

1st quarter:
... Now, I want to be perfectly clear about something: I am in no way complaining about the weather. When you run a race in the Caribbean, you know well in advance you are going to be running in warm temperatures. This is simply a reality. Runners must simply do their best to deal with this challenge and hope that the race staff does their best as well. As you will soon see, the race staff came through on their end

with flying colors.

... At the starting line, a sizeable crowd gathered consisting of, not only runners ... but also countless volunteers and a surprising number of spectators. In fact, it was a pretty darn impressive crowd showing their faces at a time I like to call O'Dark Thirty.

2nd quarter: Halfway

... As I made the turn around and began to head back, I saw a male runner and female runner approaching me from the other way. They looked totally in synch with each other and given how well they were running I assumed they would be competition for me pretty soon. Little did I know that in about 2 miles, they would pass me effortlessly, like a four-legged machine which just chewed me up and spit me out. We exchanged pleasantries as they flew by, but I was admittingly crest-fallen as the other two runners already in front of me had opened up a sizeable lead leaving me in fifth place overall. I knew that the race could get rough ahead (because of the rising sun, not the course itself, which was as flat a course as you are going to find) so I just ignored their pace as they passed me and continued on at my own clip.

... As we neared the halfway point I could hear the footsteps of the lucky bastards who were finishing the half marathon....While my shin, which had magically stopped hurting the day before the race, had started to ache again, it was not this pain that was slowing me down. Rather, the rapidly rising sun and humidity hanging in the air like a wet blanket was beginning to take its toll. I seriously envy those who do not get affected by the humidity, as it, without a doubt, simply saps me of energy. That said, I still felt relatively good here as I passed through the arch of balloons marking the halfway point. An announcer shouted everyone's name and hometown as onlookers cheered loudly.

3rd quarter:

... To top it off, not only were the liquids which were given out ice-cold (something I am sure the runners later in the day appreciated even more than I did) but full bottles were handed out along with your usual cups. I found this astounding as both Gatorade and water were handed to the runners in abundance. There was absolutely no reason why a runner could not be properly hydrated on this course. For a race only in its fifth year, this was a superb touch.

... As Julia and I made the turn, I stopped for a tall cool bottle of Gatorade for the final push and asked if it was too late to sign up for the relay. I got the desired laugh from the volunteers which gave me a spurt of energy.

4th quarter: Finish

... It is amazing what hindsight does for you. I am pretty sure that stopping for that Gatorade was probably the worst thing I could have done. For whatever reason, my legs tightened and I started to leak energy out of every pore. Moreover, Julia started to pull away from me, and other competitors, who I didn't even know were right behind me, inched closer as I headed home for the final stretch of six miles. The previously unknown competition closing in, combined with the sun, which was fully in the sky by now, both weighed down on me heavily.

... Usually my recaps end here but I have to add a few things about the rest of the race. Perhaps because I am usually on my way to the airport and therefore do not get to see the finish of most races, I have to say how impressed I am with how this race concluded its festivities. As every runner came across the finish line, the announcer would announce them by name and a huge roar would erupt from the crowd. I am not kidding. Runner after runner, all the way to the last two finishers at just over 6 hours were spurred on by a crowd which had hung around, talking and chatting and cheering. It was an awe-inspiring sight for me and one I am sure every runner was happy to be a part of.

These are the fast runners – the one's that ran hard and placed. For most of us though, we were never contenders. We arrived with other experiences, other expectations. Just to finish, for example. Or planning to make sure we had fun. And not get injured.

Some runners had more specific circumstances. Stephen Jackson celebrated his 50th birthday on Race Day and completed his first marathon. For whatever reasons they run it doesn't really matter where runners place or what time they do, you'll always see a huge sense of satisfaction on their faces when they cross the finish line.

There were many great stories and accounts of the race day. Some of these are shown here, again in the words of the runners themselves.

Training for the Half Marathon | Part 3

On the morning of the race I felt "okay". This was it, sore or not. I ran steadily at my own pace, which was faster than I trained at, but I knew that during training I had not pushed myself but had instead run comfortably and often had a bit more gas in the tank at the end. I really enjoyed my run. I felt strong and as it was the same route I trained on I had my markers. It felt weird running with so many people around as I was used to running on my own and that took some getting used to. At 11 miles I could feel myself tiring but the legs just kept going. The water stops were great. They were so enthusiastic given it was so early in the morning that it kept you going. I managed to beat my target time by 6 minutes which astounded me at the end of the race. But the main thing for me was that I actually enjoyed the whole run. My legs were tight afterwards as would be expected, but within a day that was gone. The Cayman Islands Marathon was extremely well organized and I am happy that I was able to take part in it. I am looking forward to 2007, and hopefully in the future double the distance.

My name is Derek Larner and I am a volunteer adult instructor with the Cayman Islands Cadet Corps. I ran/marched the half-marathon route wearing my cadet uniform and carried 40lbs of weight in a rucksack, which was to bring attention to the Corps. I can tell you that I hadn't done anything like that since I was in the British Army 16 years earlier. My personal goal was to run/march at the same pace as the Army; they take 2 hours to march 10 miles in full kit (30lbs of weight with a rifle). The event went very well for me. I paced each mile and got to the 10 mile mark in 1 hr 59 minutes. I kept the pace going and got to the finish line in just over 2 hrs 32 minutes. Although I felt very good doing the event, I can tell you that I had a tired and aching back for 3–4 days, had some interesting blisters on my feet from wearing boots and a sweat rash from the combat trousers I was wearing…it was all worth it. Next year, it is possible that I may try to complete the full marathon in the same kit. I will try and raise money for a worthy cause. I did manage to collect a few hundred for Pines Retirement home this time round.

At 4am my 4-year old was asking "why are you going for a run now Mummy? It's dark outside." Then she ran around the living room showing me how fast she could run. It was a great feeling lining up at the start line in George Town with all the other competitors, in the pitch black. The run felt the easiest I had ever done with all the people to run alongside and the wonderfully supportive drinks station monitors cheering us on. I was very happy with my time. So now I have achieved the half marathon the full marathon beckons. I have applied for The London Marathon in 2007 but am yet to hear if I have made it, so perhaps I will be back next December for the Cayman Islands Full marathon.

Caymanian Running

I am a Caymanian, 33 years old, and found running a couple of years ago. I fell in love with it. Two years ago I struggled to run more than 3 miles. Now I can run 8+ miles without a second thought. This year's Cayman Islands Marathon was my first attempt at a 1/2 marathon and although I trained for it, 3 weeks prior I contracted a nasty cold that turned into Bronchitis and I had to stop running. I was just completing my second course of antibiotics when the race weekend rolled around and I still had an annoying cough. But I was much better so I thought I'd just go ahead and run anyway and see how I went. I jogged all the way and finished in 2 hours 14mins, which was not the time I wanted but I was thrilled anyway as with my health and the lack of running I had done prior I felt I did myself proud! I was so touched by all the wonderful people that came out of their homes so early in the morning to stand on the road and cheer us all on – the atmosphere was wonderful and the support was really something. I am now utterly hooked, and ran my second 1/2 marathon on January 13th 2007 here in Grand Cayman for the Cancer Society in exactly 2 hours and I will run my next 1/2 on Feb 18th (the day before my 34th Birthday) in Fort Lauderdale at the A1A marathon and 1/2 marathon event. I have set myself the goal of running a half marathon every month this year and I would like to get accepted to run the New York Full marathon in November – we will see!)

A Good Hurt

I was on Team Gatorade in the Relay marathon. When I began running my left knee was really hurting me because several weeks before the marathon I sprained it. I thought I couldn't make the finishing line, but I actually did it. Then the day after I could barely stand up – both of my legs were so hurt. I was in bed day and night. But now I feel good and the pain is totally gone. It was a good experience and I plan to get involved next year if I'm still on the island.

For people out there – join us, you have nothing to lose, don't be afraid if you don't think you are physically fit.

"I have never felt so good"

To take part in the Cayman Islands Marathon 2006 was a wonderful experience. Sports have always been important in my life, although I never participated in any international event before like a Marathon. I'm from Veracruz, Mexico and for the past year I have been working on these beautiful Islands. I had been running as a hobby and when I heard about this event I decided to participate for the first time. I realize that it doesn't matter how much you prepare for an event anything can happen. Two days before the Marathon I injured my knee at work. The only thing that came to mind was if I would be able to run. I felt a little discouraged because of my knee. I tried to take care of my knee the best as I could.

I ran the half marathon. I did it! During the Marathon I realized how much courage everybody can have in order to succeed. After 1-hour and 40 minutes I saw a lady older than me running and looking very fresh. That motivated me to finish.

My knee? I forgot everything about it. By the way, I have never felt so good than that day! The Finish was so great. And to be able to receive that medal! And I give thanks to God to be able to participate and finish. (Jorge Serrano Marin (Borcha))

An Achievement I really Hadn't Imagined

In mid-October I rather spontaneously signed up to run 13 miles under the glamorous title of a half-marathon. With no prior running achievements I was quite the beginner, but thought my general 'fitness' would pull me through. My job as a waitress was becoming more and more demanding and so training didn't seem to increase quite as it should have. My training never sur-

passed 4 miles! My participation in this race was definitely in question and so my response to others was that I wasn't running anymore. As a last minute effort to join in somehow I tried to change my distance to the relay ~ 6 miles but without any team members it was not possible and so it seemed almost definite I was not running. Saturday evening when planning a night out with my friends I considered I would try running some of it. With work at 2pm on Sunday I wasn't sure I should realistically take part but the idea of catching glimpses of runners racing past my house made me rethink what I was giving up. I decided to run the 13 miles I had signed up for and told my parents at 9.30pm on Saturday. Much to my concerned mother's disapproval I set the alarm for 4am. Nerves and excitement got me out of bed by 3am and I headed down to the harbour for the start. I met up with a friend who was running the relay and we set off together. The race was tough but the atmosphere created by the runners and officials was great. All the supporters and helpers made the event such a successful morning and really kept beginner runners like myself going mile after mile. Finishing the 13 miles, with my friend (who ran an extra 6 miles with me 'because she had to pick up her car from town'), was an achievement I really hadn't imagined I'd complete, and I think I've sparked a new interest that I hope I can improve on next year. Thanks so much to the organizers for making things run so smoothly – no pun intended, and to the physiotherapists – the free massage was ace!
(Sophie Benbow, 18-years old).

I felt the weather was perfect, although a little more breeze would not have hurt anyone. The course itself was spectacular and the people along the course could not have been more motivating. The experience will be cherished forever and what a way to enter into my 40's – thank you for the opportunity to be a part of such a wonderful event!

Gearing Up | Part 2

On Saturday before the big day we both encountered a little problem with both our right legs! I got stung by a jellyfish and Ceri leaned on her mothers flattening irons!! What a pair!! We were ready!! We decided to go at the back of the pack and take it easy – saving the best for last! We had massive support along the way from family and friends which, without all the support the training would have been impossible. We were off! The weather was perfect, not too hot, not too cold and no rain. The buzz of the morning was fantastic and the turn out excellent. Both of us could not believe we were finally doing the race, all the build up and training and here we are actually running a half marathon – who'd have thought! We were very fortunate with our training and we had run on most of the course. Our longest run was 10 miles in our training so when we got to mile 11 we were starting to feel it in our legs! At mile 12 we started to feel much better and we were just around the corner from the finish. Everyone was there to watch us run across the finish line, the clock said 2 hours 43 minutes and 22 seconds! Whooooww!!!! We did it. And we did it 30 minutes quicker than we had thought and we didn't walk at all!!! Our legs were like jelly but we felt amazing and so happy to have been part of the Cayman Islands Half Marathon. Next year...................... Hummmmm maybe!

The Canadian Connection

"Yes it was a wonderful run and our family in Grand Cayman (who are not runners) could not believe that friends would get up at 4am, in the dark, to run at 5am, in the snow to support another friend."

While the Canadian couple – Mike and Stephanie Jones from Clippity Clop

Farm in Richards Landing, Ontario Canada, – got up to run in the 5am Cayman Islands marathon, their friends back home in Ontario decided to run the same distance at the same time. The major difference of course was that in Ontario where their friends ran there was snow on the ground. So for Mike and Stephanie it was great to be somewhere else while Ontario experienced the snow. As the photographs show, there is a completely different running kit for winter running. But their friends ran anyway. Even though they weren't able to be in the Cayman Islands they at least shared the experience, albeit in a much more wintery context.

29th Sep 06: We arrive in Grand Cayman. 'It's a bit hot!' Do I still want to enter the half marathon?

Oct 06: I went out for my first Caribbean run. I thought I was out early enough to beat the sun (7am). No, you've got to be out earlier than that! I soon gave up morning running and went out in the evening instead – much better.

19th Nov 06: My first Caribbean race – the Pirates Week 10K. Luckily it was grey and overcast. It even had a drop of rain to keep us cool. Cool? It was still hot! By now I had entered the half marathon. What have I let myself in for?

2nd Dec 06: The time has arrived to collect my race welcome pack, there's no escaping now. What a great welcome pack, lots of goodies. But I see T-shirt sizing is a world-wide problem with my massive small T-shirt! I check the route and have a rough idea where we'll be going. Not that it's a concern; there will be plenty of people for me to follow! We go to Breezes Pasta Party then its home to get my kit ready and have an early night.

3rd Dec 06: Race Day: Up at 4am – on a day off as well – must be mad! Had my 2 slices of toast then we drove to the start. There was a good atmosphere at the start, and most importantly Breezes was open for the pre-race toilet stop! Then ... PANIC!

Two minutes before the start I tugged my time chip to check it was secure and it came off. I couldn't do it back up so I was flapping looking for a velcro band, luckily I found the stall and got my chip secured around my ankle just in time for the final countdown.

5am on the dot we were off. Still hot that time of day. I spotted Colin at the side of the road cheering me on. I plodded along South Sound. Didn't realize how long that road was. So dark in places as well, luckily I didn't go down one of Cayman's potholes!

I soon came across the first water stop so I took my drink and had a walk. My theory was to do the run / walk method. Walk for 1 minute after taking a drink then run. It's frustrating over the first few miles as most people over take you, but it was working well by the half way point.

There were a few brave souls up early cheering us on. I tried to raise a smile and a wave of thanks to these kind people. But nowhere near as many supporters as the London Marathon - thank goodness. I much prefer running when it's quieter.

The water stations were well placed. I kept my eyes out for a decorated station so I could nominate one for the Water Stop Challenge. It was very bleak till I reached the Mexican Water Stop. Very impressive. We even had ice cubes in our drinks! They got my vote.

Then it was back along South Sound where I came under attack from loads of midges! I could feel them hitting me; conversations stopped due to the fear of swallowing them! Luckily they quickly disappeared and the sun started to come up.

I checked my watch. I was on course to finish in less than 2 hours – before the sun got too high. That was until I reached mile 10. I'm sure mile 10 to 11 was the longest mile on the course! My legs were heavy and my plodding got slower! I then had to keep my eye on my watch and force myself on. I really wanted to finish in under 2 hours.

I came along Hospital Road and was greeted by crazy fruits outside the police station. I took my last drink and had my last walk. Then it was full steam ahead to the end! Someone who had already finished shouted 'only 200m to go'. Great, I thought, I can do this. I sped up (slightly) although those last 200m went on for ages. But then the FINISH banner came in sight. HORRAY I've done it! And I got a great turtle medal to prove it!

I went straight through to the massage tent. I'm sure those poor ladies had the worst job of the day! I had a great leg massage then celebrated with a beer. That was a first. I've never seen beer at the end of a race before, but it's good to try new things!

We stayed to watch the first marathon finishers come home and was pleased to cheer the female winner in. Then it was home to log on to the Haverhill Running Club web site; up-date them on my progress and encourage them to come over next year.

Memories

On race morning I was wide awake and so excited to be there with people from all over the world. After the starting gun, as soon as we began down South Church St. all was quiet. Everyone ran silently, either listening to their I-pods or just alone in their own thoughts. I breathed in the sweet smell of the flowers and sea air, listened to the chickens, remembered times of riding my bicycle down this road in the dark, sneaking home from a late night out or getting to work extra early. I marvelled at how most everything had been so beautifully rebuilt since my last visit just after Hurricane Ivan, and that which wasn't was now covered with lush green vines. I passed apartments where I had once lived, empty lots where once my favourite watering holes had been, dive-shops where I imagined jumping in and exploring reefs I remembered so well. The miles passed quickly as I bounced from water station to water station giggling at all the creative competitors. By mile 11 my joyous trip down memory lane had faded into a trudge up Walker's Road but it didn't bother me to walk for a while or even that my time wasn't anything close to award winning. I still crossed the finish line with a happy smile and even walked another couple of miles up Seven Mile Beach back to my hotel afterwards. The next day I went scuba diving out East End way and was again rewarded by Cayman's exquisite walls and sea life – even a hammerhead shark swam by!

While life in the Bahamas is fabulous I always enjoy trips back to Cayman and am looking for a triathlon to do on my next visit!

"It's hot and humid! Duh, it's a Caribbean island. No it's really hot and humid!! Drink more and keep running..."

What Have I Signed Myself Up For?

In the days and hours leading up to the start of the race, I began to have a few worries about what I'd signed myself up for. While I've done distance training in the past, none of it had ever been as far as a half marathon. Once the race started, I let everyone else run on ahead of me. I tried to settle into a comfortable walking pace and concentrate on getting to the first mile marker. I was gunning for a 31⁄4 to 31⁄2 hour run time (roughly 15 minutes per mile, give or take a few minutes for bathroom breaks, fatigue etc). I didn't really notice the miles as the race went on, as the course was more than familiar to me, as I used to ride my bike along the route. When I got to the half way mark, it didn't even phase me that I'd made it half way and I still had to go back from whence I came. However, once I got to within 2 miles of the finish, I started to feel fatigued – my hips hurt and my thighs started to get crampy. And at mile 12, I started to get cranky because I was so very tired and didn't know the exact route to the finish (go figure, seeing as I've lived here for 18 months!). At the end, I didn't know whether to laugh or cry because I'd made it through with a little less than 10 minutes to spare from my estimated time. I ended up finding a plastic patio chair, parked my caboose and texted my roomate on my cell phone.

Just Start With It

Being a South African, I have run most of my marathons in this beautiful country with undulating terrain and sunny skies. It was while running The Two Oceans, a challenging ultra marathon, where the story of my ritual began. This was the first race that Dad was not going to be able to stand on the roadside and pass me my favourite chocolate and shout words of encouragement, as he had another pressing engagement. Instead he had carved a piece of driftwood that fitted perfectly into my hand so that I could carry it and know that he was with me. Knowing that I found carrying objects while running cumbersome, he insisted that I did not have to carry it all the way but I was to, "Just start with it."

I crossed the finish line with my driftwood firmly placed in my hand. Needless to say, when I left South Africa for the Cayman Islands the first thing in my suitcase was my driftwood (it was the next best thing to packing Dad), then came the trainers. The morning of The Cayman Island's Marathon finally dawned and it was not only the training but Dad's driftwood that helped me cross the finish line. Thanks Dad, the driftwood is placed right next to my medal, until the next one. Unless of course, you are planning to be there!

From a Family Supporter

My daughter, who is in her late twenties, has lived in Grand Cayman since her marriage in 2002. My brother, at 60, has run a number of races but in the northern climes of the US, mostly Maryland and New Jersey. For the family to meet in Grand Cayman, and cheer them on, seemed a great way to get together. Ivan set back our plans a bit, and when we finally succeeded in 2006 not all the family could make it. But those of us who did had a fabulous time. Personally, I am not a road racer but I have attended a number of races over the years to cheer on family members so I have other races to compare with the Cayman Marathon. The intimacy of the race may be one of the best aspects. We, racers and supporters, were greeted at the airport as if we were celebrities. Registration went like clockwork. And the goody bag had without a doubt the niftiest fan I have ever seen. The race bus was only ten minutes late and the race itself started exactly on time.

From the Veteran Racer

At sixty, Ralph is an experienced road runner with excess of 1,000 racing miles. As one of the 78 off islanders, he told me that Cayman was one of the most exotic locals he has ever run. The roosters, the ocean sounds, the frying of plantain and fritters all made for a colorful background. To entertain himself he started identifying the accents of the other runners which included British, Irish, Australian and Kiwi. The heat was a major drawback for him. He also found the dark streets at 5 AM somewhat perilous, but not enough to keep him from coming back. He is already planning on a longer visit next year to become more comfortable with the heat (Note: Ralph finished in the top of his age group).

Marion is a multidimensional athlete combining body building and running. Since she lives in the Cayman Islands now, she is used to the exotic locale. Marion loved the water stops. She told me they really helped the racers pass the time and the enthusiasm was inspiring in some areas where there were no observers. In particular, she loved the Grey's Anatomy nurses. (Note: Marion was the third woman to finish).

'24 Hours'
Saturday afternoon:

Confused. Should I laze by pool or on beach?

Decide to do both, but not at same time.

Mentally prepare for race horizontally. Take a break – cleanse mind and spirit with swims. Lie down in ocean.

No guilt about doing nothing.

Two drinks with umbrellas placed in front of me.

Make effort to walk to pasta party 25 minutes away.

It's hot and humid. Like a tropical island.

Pasta Party veritable United Nations. Decide not to solve world's problems. Concentrate instead on our own.

Get more nervous about race.

Walk back to Hotel. No-one has turned thermostat down.

Wander accidentally past Jazz Festival. Drawn in like magnet.

Amazing music. Forget I'm running at 5am. Crowd grows through night. Drink water. There is a buzz.

10:30pm. Discover buzz is in my ears. Drink more water.

Natalie Cole finally comes on stage. Explosion of sound. Cuba and Jamaica hear Natalie.

11:30pm. Must go. Have race at 5am.

Natalie stays. Perhaps not racing in AM?

Race Day:

3:55am. Alarm goes off. Why? Hit snooze.

3:58am. Alarm goes off. Start to get idea. Hit snooze.

4:01am. Alarm goes off. Oh, Got it.

4:02am. Hotel wake-up call.

4:03am. Make coffee.

4:07am. Hotel wake-up call. Don't believe me from first call.

4:12am. Hotel wake-up call. Yes, I'm sure, thanks.

4:20am. Shower.

4:25am. Begin to wake-up. Eat energy bar. Put all running gear on. I think.

4:30am. Catch shuttle bus to start-line. Meet others on bus. Share 'hoped for' finishing times. Turns-out we are all dreaming.

4:40am. Bus makes way to start-line solely on nervous energy of passengers.

4:41am. Runners, friends and family mingle with volunteers and organizers. Music. Darkness. Festive. Last minute preparations and thoughts. Am Zombie with an excuse.

4:55am. What am I doing?

4:56am. Assemble with others behind Start Line. Put Lifeline MP3 player on.

5:00am. Bang! We're off.

5:01am. Adrenalin rush.

5:03am. Soaking in sweat. My own.

5:03am. Smiles, concentration, darkness. Roosters.

5:20am. Am in the groove. Feels good. Love the music.

6:00am. 1/4 of the way. Still feels good despite hot and humid. Am on track for 4-hour marathon. Can I do it?

6:50am. Meet runner from Hotel. Not looking good, not sounding good. Says he's not good. Start to worry.

7:00am. Something possibly wrong with distance on Polar watch. Says am half-way already at 12.5 miles. Is distance of course wrong?

7:12am. Reach real Halfway. Feel good but not as good as before.

7:20am. Sun coming out. Not good.

7:25am. Sun getting hotter.

7:26am. Body systems losing power. Imminent shut-down.

7:45am. Crisis. MP3 music gets scratchy and intermittent, losing sound.

7:46am. Become audio technician for next 30 minutes. Use valuable scarce energy turning MP3 player on and off 100 times. But no hope for Polar watch, which is lying to me now.

8:15am: Plod like Sloth on valium.

8:18am: Turtle walks past.

8:20am. Decide silence better than scratchy noise. Put MP3 away. Now what?

8:25am. Reach 3/4 mark. 4-hour marathon? No chance unless Jerry on motorbike picks me up.

8:26am. Begin longest 6 1/2 miles of my life. Why does sun get hotter?

8:30am. Meet-up with fellow runner. Share longest 6 1/2 miles of my life. Start run-walk strategy.

8:35am. Talk incoherently. Raise possibility with other runner that course is too long. He smiles and nods head. Must think I'm in LaLa land.

8:36am. Am I in LaLa Land?

8:37am. It's hot in LaLa Land.

8:45am. See mirage of taller buildings 500 miles away where Finish Line waits.

8:50am. Run-walk becomes walk-run. Still moving in right direction with brother-in-arms. Legs gone. Am now dragging heavy lead weights around course.

9:00am. Don't recognize part of course apparently just ran over earlier. Are we lost?

9:15am. 'Not long now – almost there' say's spectator. Good one.

9:20am. Getting closer to tall buildings. They now look real. There is hope.

9:25am. Conversations with fellow runner priceless. Tell life story.

9:30am. Other runner now runs ahead of me. What?

9:30am. Run to catch-up with fellow runner. Why?

9:32am. Can't run any more. Sloth on valium returns to body. Run anyway.

9:34am. Catch-up with fellow runner.

9:34am. Run to finish line with smile on face borrowed from spectator. Feels like sprint. Can't feel body below waist. Mistakenly think am lifting feet off ground. But realise legs just painted on now.

9:35am. Cross finish-line together with fellow runner.

9:35am. Receive medal. Smile lots. Weight of medal pulls body closer to ground.

9:36am. Stop moving. Legs start to seize up.

9:40am. Wait in short line for massage.

9:41am. Line not short enough. Sit down in line.

9:42am. Get moved up line and on to massage table.

9:43am. Ahhhhhhhhhhh.

10:00am. Sinks in. I've done it. Tough one. Am very proud. Start thinking of next marathon. Roll gently off massage table.

Thereafter: Drink and eat as if come out of 30 days in desert. Everyone proud of everyone else. All share congratulations, hugs, stories, contact information. Special moment, special memories shared. MP3 still not working.

Chapter 9

Finished!

In the final stretch of the course we weave our way through the central George Town streets. We turn the last corner and see the finish line a couple of hundred yards away. This is a great feeling. Suddenly the end is in sight and we know we've 'done it'!

Onlookers, volunteers, friends and family, and runners who have finished cheer us along. The memory of these last moments gets a little blurry. It all happens quickly, even if by now we're running or walking at a snail's pace. I wanted to look strong and full of energy when I finished, which was the opposite of how I felt.

The training programs say not to finish with a sprint because of the risk of injury. Instead, finish with good relaxed form. That's the theory. Although I thought I might have been doing this, when I saw my finish line photos it looked quite different.

We finally finish. There is a mental jig-of-joy. However we may feel, no one can take away the fact that we've completed what we set out to do. Our names are called out over the loud speaker as we cross the line. Immediately after, a finisher's medal is placed around our necks. This is the symbol of accomplishment. It's an extremely proud moment.

In those next few moments we're congratulated by people we know and people we don't know. Complete strangers shake our hand, or give us a hug. Photos are taken, and continue to be taken for the rest of the morning. It starts to sink in. We've finished. Our bodies begin to remind us of what just happened over the previous few hours. In my case it was saying 'go to the massage tent', which is exactly what I did.

The complementary massage service was provided by Focus Hair and Beauty, operated by Charlene Barnes. As Charlene commented afterwards, "The minute you take pain away from someone you feel really good about what you're doing".

The massage therapists were in a Tent at the finish line intersection from 6am through to 11am, providing relief to dozens of runners. The aim was to get runners as comfortable as possible, recognizing that their bodies had been through a lot.

Only so much is possible immediately after a marathon as the muscles are very tender to say the least. In the massage itself, which lasted around 15 minutes or so, Gemma or Karen would work on the more painful parts of your body. Typically it was the legs – especially the calves, quadriceps and hamstring muscles, and also the feet and neck.

In my case it was my legs. They felt as if they'd been run over by a Cayman Airways Boeing 737. It was challenging just to stand. But what a huge difference the massage made.

The massage therapists were having lots of fun, and made it fun – they had music playing and there was plenty to talk and laugh about. But they did the serious massage work too, non-stop throughout the morning.

I certainly felt good about what they were doing. I could've easily stayed on the massage table all morning. Perhaps forever. The worst part was knowing that the massage would come to an end.

And it did. I spent the rest of the morning sitting in the sun on the side of the street, drinking and talking to other runners and their friends and family members. Despite the aches and pains there was a terrific relaxed intimate feeling all around. Everyone milled around the intersection and Breezes by the Bay, talking about the run, possible next runs, other experiences in previous races, injuries, muscle stiffness, and training, and just getting to know one another a bit better.

And we contemplate. We learn a lot about other people as well as about ourselves in these moments. Despite how our bodies may feel, we have a wonderful time, often with people who were complete strangers earlier in the day. We may feel sore and tired but we feel alive.

All the while we make sure we drink plenty of fluids and eat something to begin the process of restoring our energy levels. We also walk around a bit to cool down, help release any lactic acid build up, and to ease our muscles into recovery.

We wait for the final runners to come in and then the Awards ceremony begins. All those who placed, as well as the top water stations, go up on stage to receive their awards. Shortly afterwards, the event is officially 'over' and everyone disappears into the Island once more.

For the organizers, but at least with the help of volunteers, everything must now be taken down and packed up so that the Island can return to its normal routine. By the end of the day there is little to suggest the marathon has been run.

There is immense relief and an enormous amount of satisfaction for the organizers. Everyone has had a great experience. Many wonderful memories are made. As Steve Kurtenbach from AllSportCentral commented; "it's extremely gratifying when you see the jubilation from people and they come and thank-you for all the work that you've done".

By later in the day, the biggest clue that there had been a marathon event is the runners themselves, many of whom are now walking a little slower, or perhaps limping in some cases. Some runners continue to wear their medals for the rest of the day, and even the day afterwards.

In the days immediately following the event the organizers will meet and start planning for the 2007 Cayman Islands Marathon.

For many of the runners who were visiting from off the island this is when the relaxation can really begin. There's plenty to do asides from running, as the runners themselves pointed out. We'll talk about these things next, in the final chapter.

Chapter 10

The Cayman Islands: More Than Just a Marathon

In many ways you can be quite busy relaxing. The nice thing about the Islands is that you have the choice. You can simply sleep on the beach or by the pool, or be more active and go swimming, diving, snorkelling, riding, parasailing 400 feet high, ... or jet-skiing... virtually anything is possible. I'd suggest running, but ...

Visitors can experience the turtle farm, or the butterfly farm, swim with Stingrays, take a ride in the Atlantis submarine, walk through gardens and woodlands, catch up on some history, take in the views from Rum Point, and shop!

Or do nothing.

Average water temperatures are about 80 degrees Fahrenheit, so it's perfect for weary aching muscles after a run. As the waters are teeming with fish, snorkelling is a great activity for all ages. There are dozens of dive operators and numerous sites for diving around the island, including shipwrecks, coral reefs to explore and deep wall dives.

And somewhere in-between diving and snorkelling is the ability to go to depths of up to 100 feet, day or night, in an air conditioned submarine. Or ride the Nautilus – a 60-passenger semi-submarine that cruises five feet below the surface. There's also a 'Bubble Sub'- a small battery operated, 360 degree glass bubble submarine which seats two people.

Biodiversity is a word increasingly associated with the Cayman Islands. If you love the outdoors there's plenty to look for. There are over 700 species of plants and 380 species of fish. Over 200 species of birds have been recorded on the island, including 50 resident species.

And then there are the more unique attractions like the Stingrays and turtles. Perhaps the most unique experience is to swim with Stingrays. This is possible either at Stingray City or at the Stingray Sandbar.

Stingray City is not your typical city. In fact it's not a city at all but rather a specific place where Stingrays congregate in the hope of getting some food. Many years ago a local fisherman noticed stingrays swimming around his boat when he was throwing scraps overboard. Some Divers started to feed them by hand and now it has become a major tourist attraction.

But it is a very amazing low key natural experience.

You are taken out on a boat to the 'City', which is close to the reef. You then simply go into about 12 foot deep of water and swim with the Stingrays.

The Stingrays are curious and feel like Velvet, or mushrooms, as they brush-up alongside you. They're always interested in eating, of course, typically squid, and will suck the squid from your hand with what feels like a high-powered vacuum cleaner. The more adventurous swimmers may choose to hold the Stingrays in their hands. Although they do have a Barb on their tails for defensive purposes, it's very safe to swim with them and hold them. Especially because they know that there is always a good chance of being fed. In fact, they are very friendly and like being petted. The tour operators have given many of them names.

Another highlight is a visit to the Cayman Turtle Farm, the only one of its kind in the world. For some of us, this brings back memories of the race just run. There are about 14,000 green sea turtles living at the Farm, some of which are up to 600 pounds in size. These turtles take between 15-50 years to mature and can live to 100 years old. The Farm has an active release program. Visitors can see them being fed in the mornings and afternoons.

If such places are of no interest to you, you can go to Hell.

Really.

In an area of West Bay on Grand Cayman Island there is a rugged outcrop of eroded limestone and dolomite that is reputed to be over 1.5 million years old. A postcard from the nearby 'Devils Hang-Out' store explains that it was named 'Hell' after a commissioner from England in the 1930s shot at, and missed, a bird in the rocks and cried out 'Oh Hell'. Somehow this stuck over time. It's quite the thing to go to the local Post Office and have your postcard or letter stamped with a Hell postmark.

If none of these things interest you it is hard to resist the beach atmosphere. All beaches in the Cayman Islands are public. The beaches are accessible to everyone all around the island, including the famous Seven Mile beach, which is really about 5 1/2 miles long. You can spend hours just wandering around the beaches. They can be quiet and secluded or just the opposite. Again, the choice is yours.

We could go on about everything you can do on the islands but that's not the point. The runners said that the activities mentioned here, or just relaxing on the beaches, were what stood out for them during their visit.

For some, seeing these sights was the reward for the goal accomplished; for the race that was run – a great way to combine their passion and enthusiasm for running with a vacation.

Chapter 11

Final Words

And so the Cayman Islands marathon is over for another year. For many runners, volunteers and onlookers it was an inspirational event.

There's many messages that we can take from the experiences of the runners in the Cayman Islands. Here's eight key messages:

1.Have fun

It was clear that the runners had fun while racing and in the Cayman Islands more generally. In the Introduction I said that it's "a long way. Especially at the End". It may not exactly sound like 'fun' but once you've completed the run the satisfaction is immense, and you quickly forget the more challenging aspects of the run. Thinking about having fun and being less concerned about a specific finish time will make it a more enjoyable experience.

2.Set goals

Distance runners set goals. They have lengthy training programs to work with and need to be goal-oriented if they're to achieve what they set out to do. That's in part why it's so rewarding to have completed a marathon or half-marathon.

3.Start small and build up

If you've not run long distances before or run much at all, set realistic goals to attain, start small and build up. It works. And then reward yourself! Run/walk programs work really well for Beginners.

4.Believe in yourself

Some days you'll feel like nothing is working and you can barely run to the end of the driveway. But have faith in yourself and be comforted by the fact that if you stick to the training program as best you can, eventually you'll have greater capacity to run further and further, and feel better about yourself along the way! Stay the course.

5.Avoid injury

No point trying to be a hero in training. Doing more miles in training does not necessarily make you a better runner. Run smart, and avoid injuries. Gradually build-up the distance you run. If something hurts and is getting worse, listen to what your body is saying and rest. You don't have to rigidly adhere to a program if it means you are damaging your body as a result.

6.Get proper running shoes

It's one of the cheapest forms of exercise. As the Cayman Island marathoners said, one of the most important things to do is to get really good running shoes. After that, there's not much more cost involved. Talk to the Sports and Running stores and learn what types of running shoes will work best for your feet. Money spent on good running shoes will improve your running experience and decrease the chance of injury.

7.Enjoy every moment of your first long distance race

As was mentioned earlier, if it's not enjoyable why do it? Don't become obsessed with your finish time – you can work on times later. Run to enjoy the experience.

8.Have fun

I know. It was #1 on the list. But it's so important that it's worth two appearances. It's hard not to have fun when you run in a great location.

The good news – and I hope it shows from the comments by the runners – and indeed the photographs – is that running a half or full marathon in the Cayman Islands is an enjoyable, memorable marathon experience.

In fact, many of the 2006 runners have said they would like to return and run the marathon or half marathon again in 2007. If the words and images from the 2006 runners and volunteers in this book are anything to go by, many great experiences will continue to be shared in future Cayman Islands marathons.

As a destination marathon, the future looks extremely promising.

Books referenced in the text:

Clark, N. (2003). Nancy Clark's Sports Nutrition Guidebook (3rd edition). Human Kinetics. Champaign, Illinois US.

Noakes, T. (2003). The Lore of Running. (4th Edition). Human Kinetics. Champaign, Illinois US.

Switzer, K and R. Robinson (2006). 26.2 Marathon Stories. Madison Press Books. Toronto.

Cayman Islands Marathon Website
www. caymanislandsmarathon.com/

Appendices

Saying Thanks

This book has presented accounts of the marathon experience through the words of the runners, volunteers and organizers. Many runners also wrote in to express their thanks for the event. These are included below.

"In closing, I would like to again offer my sincere congratulations to you and all the volunteers for a wonderful job. Can't wait for next year's race!!"

"I would also like to add that I think the Cayman Islands Marathon was one of the best run/organized races in which I have participated. The water stops were frequent and prepared (i.e. they never ran out of anything). The aid provided was outstanding and the course was outstanding. I have run two full marathons and, including Cayman, 5 half-marathons. The race director and staff should be HIGHLY commended. The only disappointment was that there was no Exposition. I attribute this to the fact that there were simply not enough runners to attract vendors - it was not economically feasible for them to attend. In the future, I hope this wonderful and well run marathon grows in popularity such that vendors see the value of supporting it with great alacrity."

"Thanks for this wonderful event. This was my first half marathon and I thought it was very well organized. The frequent water stops were really appreciated and made the run a lot more pleasant. I really liked your idea of having a water stop competition as it also gave encouragement and was a lot of fun."

"The marathon was so well organized and attended....awesome and impressive! I ran with my fellow RE/MAX Power House gals and we enjoyed the event immensely as a relay team. Next time a couple of us are going to go for the half marathon! You have inspired me to become more or a runner and less of a walker! Great cause, great event!
CONGRATULATIONS!

Kass Canada Coleman
RE/MAX Cayman Islands"

"On behalf of the Commandant and all other members of the Cayman Islands Cadet Corps, we would like to express sincere thanks to you for your participation. The atmosphere of camaraderie and the festive mood which was taken to the volunteerism and other participation was very evident.

Many thanks.

Ricardo O. Henry
Captain
Adjutant Training Officer
HQ Cayman Islands Cadet Corps"

"Both of my runners talked endlessly about the water stops and the amount of effort the good folks who manned them put out. The costumes, the cheering, the enthusiasm all made the race so special."

"I have never before attended a race that gave anything to the spectators. Again the size and intimacy may have worked in our favor but I very much appreciated the free pastries, fruit and really decent coffee. Breezes by the Bay also let folks sit on their balcony and watch the race even if you weren't buying anything. It made me feel included and I appreciate that. I also have to mention the classy port-a-loos and the fact that the announcers really made an effort to broadcast everyone's name as they came in. Now if they only would incorporate a two mile health walk, I could participate also.'"

"The race course was simply outstanding. It was a runner's dream. While the heat and humidity presented a challenge, especially for me coming from a much cooler climate (i.e. leaving a snow storm) the course support was beyond outstanding; the organization was the most effective that I have seen and I would highly recommend that anyone who enjoys running and wants to see paradise sign up for the next marathon or 1/2 marathon put on by your organization."

"While not "competitive" in terms of being a world-class athlete, by any means, I do it for enjoyment and to stay in shape. All-in-all, based upon what I consider to be my extensive experience with chip timed races, I would give the Cayman Marathon a score of 9 on a scale of 1-10. The one point deduction is made only because of the lacking expo, which was due to no fault of the Cayman Marathon organizers. So, in summary, *GREAT JOB*! As a runner I truly appreciate all the efforts put forth by you and your assistants."

"The 106.1 KISS FM crew were extremely proud to promote and support the Cayman Islands Marathon which was in aid of two great causes. The Cayman Islands Cadet Corps and the Cayman Islands Cancer Society. Everyone at the KISS water stand had a great day cheering the runners on and keeping them well hydrated. 106.1 KISS FM's on-air host, 'Love King' Aldo also enjoyed giving any willing volunteers a good luck kiss to boost them on their way! Our four 106.1 KISS FM runners, who braved the challenge, managed to complete the run in an impressive 4:06:14. We'd like to thank the organizers for letting us be a part of such a great community event."

"First of all, I would like to congratulate you and all the other people involved in the organisation of this year's race. I have run in numerous half marathons over the years and can honestly say that this one is in the top 2 or 3. It was very well planned, the route was beautiful, and above all the water stations and the volunteers that manned them were absolutely fabulous. There was no need to carry any extra fluids as the stations were about every mile. The people were "high fiving" us as we passed the stations, singing and cheering us on. Next year I am hoping to run the full marathon, the only reason I didn't this year was because I was concerned about the humidity and heat, but it turned out it was no problem at all."

I am in the personal habit of collecting a running hat from each marathon or 1/2 marathon that I run ... as a momento. Cayman did not offer that option because minimal participation did not make such efforts economically viable to vendors. However, one of the marathon organizers took my information and specifically ... JUST FOR ME ... had two running hats made with the logo used on the finisher's medals. Now, that is service and support! I appreciate the incredible willingness of your team to go well above and beyond any "duty" to specifically have the hats made for me. It speaks volumes about how much you care about the runners and the success of the race. THANK YOU!"

The Sponsors

The 2006 Cayman Islands Marathon was sponsored by the following organizations:

Digicel

Cayman Islands Department of Tourism

Deloitte

Cayman National

Breezes By The Bay Restaurant (Official Marathon Party Zone)

106.1 KISS FM (Official Radio Station)

Cayman Airways

Flowers Bottled Water (Official Water)

Gatorade (Official Sports Drink)

Grand Cayman Marriott Beach Resort (Official Hotel)

TAG Heuer

Final Touch

Butterfield Bank

Audi

CUC

RE/MAX Cayman Islands

Generali

Admiral

KPMG

Red Sail Sports

Island Companies

Pepsi

AllSport Central

Kelly Holding

Race Participants

2006 Cayman Islands Half Marathon Finishers
Men

Acker, Marius (Grand Cayman)

Appleton, Kevin Durham (US – New Hampshire)

Banks, Frank (Grand Cayman)

Bernard, Stephen (Grand Cayman)

Bird, Stephen (Grand Cayman)

Bloomrosen, Allen (Grand Cayman)

Boisvert, Daniel (Grand Cayman)

Bonner, Andy (Grand Cayman)

Braich, Balbinder (Grand Cayman)

Brewster, Christopher (Grand Cayman)

Browne, Mark (Grand Cayman)

Burbidge, Michael (Grand Cayman)

Burd, Damon (US – North Carolina)

Burr, Lindsay (Grand Cayman)

Chionopoulos, Michael (US – Oklahoma)

Chong, Kingsley (Grand Cayman)

Citron, Gary (US – New Jersey)

Cortellassi, Frank (US – Illinois)

Cotton, David (US – Illinois)

Davis, Bruce (Grand Cayman)

Dietz, James (US – New York)

Dube, Sylvester (Grand Cayman)

Dube, Vumindaba (Grand Cayman)

Easdon, Chris (Grand Cayman)

Ebers, Jim (US – Illinois)

Erceg, Joseph (Grand Cayman)

Fajette, Walter (Grand Cayman)

Farley, Jarrod (Grand Cayman)

Gaffigan, Dean (Grand Cayman)

Gammage, Tom (Grand Cayman)

Garcellano, Liberato (Grand Cayman)

Giacomelli, Paolo ((Grand Cayman)

Gibbs, Jonty (Grand Cayman)

Hackenberg, Patrick (Grand Cayman)

Hall, Mike (Grand Cayman)

Hanekom, Jp (Grand Cayman)

Haq, Bushra (Grand Cayman)

Hydes, Timmy (Grand Cayman)

Jones, Michael (Canada – Ontario)

Jones, Richard (US – Illinois)

Kahlow, Edward (Grand Cayman)

Kariya, Ash (Grand Cayman)

Kerr, Blair (Grand Cayman)

Kirkconnell, Wayne (Grand Cayman)

Krys, Kenneth (Grand Cayman)

Larner, Derek (Grand Cayman)

Lecanda, Gustavo (Grand Cayman)

Lee, Ivan (Grand Cayman)

Lillie, Ralph (US – Maryland)

Lindsay, Trevor (Grand Cayman)

Macdonald, David (Grand Cayman)

MacMillan, Roger (Canada – Alberta)

Mallek, Lee (Grand Cayman)

Manning, Guy (Grand Cayman)

McCallum, Pat (Grand Cayman)

McVeigh, Jim (Grand Cayman)

Mernett, Glen (Grand Cayman)

Michalski, Joe (Grand Cayman)

Miller, Clifene (Grand Cayman)

Mirica, George (Grand Cayman)

Muchangi, Samuel (Grand Cayman)

Munro, Alastair (Grand Cayman)

Napierala, Marco (Germany)

Nieuwenhuis, Henk (Grand Cayman)

Nissar, Fredrik (Grand Cayman)

Njogu, Paul (Grand Cayman)

Nyaberi, Joshua (Grand Cayman)

Petyt, Terry (Grand Cayman)

Phillips, Simon (Grand Cayman)

Polloni, Paolo (Grand Cayman)

Portugal, James (Grand Cayman)

Reed, Stuart (Grand Cayman)

Relly, Tristan (Grand Cayman)

Richardson, Michael (Grand Cayman)

Roney, Stephen (Grand Cayman)

Schofield, Andrew (Grand Cayman)

Schnaufer, Mark (Grand Cayman)

Serrano, Jorge (Grand Cayman)

Shingler, Todd (US – Illinois)

Singleton, Richie (Grand Cayman)

Somerville, John (Grand Cayman)

Somerville, Scott (Grand Cayman)

Sordinelli , Fabio (Grand Cayman)

Spratt, Peter (Grand Cayman)

Surrey, Steve (Grand Cayman)

Sutcliffe, Philip (Grand Cayman)

Tedd, Martin (Grand Cayman)

Thacker, Gareth (Grand Cayman)

Touhey, Brendan (Grand Cayman)

Tremel, Philippe (Grand Cayman)

Walker, Dave (Grand Cayman)

Walker, Matthew (Grand Cayman)

Walsh, Kieran (Grand Cayman)

Watson, Simon (Grand Cayman)

Webster, William (Canada – Ontario)

Wilson, Gary (Grand Cayman)

Vitorino, Jacobo (Grand Cayman)

Wertz , Marcus (US – Texas)

Yeomans, Rodger (Grand Cayman)

Yunker, Daniel (Grand Cayman)

Women

Allard, Vanessa (Grand Cayman)
Arch, Michelle (Grand Cayman)
Arie, Cynthia (Grand Cayman)
Bailey, Anna-Lise (Grand Cayman)
Balderamos, Nora (Grand Cayman)
Banks, Sharon (Grand Cayman)
Beales-Hart, Charlotte (Grand Cayman)
Benbow, Sophie (Grand Cayman)
Beaudet, Stephanie (Grand Cayman)
Bowen, Kim (Grand Cayman)
Brenton, Wanda (Grand Cayman)
Brereton, Penny (Grand Cayman)
Brereton, Tammy (Wales)
Carroll, Kimberly (Grand Cayman)
Castro, Sally (Grand Cayman)
Chickris, Nicole (Grand Cayman)
Colgan, Linda (Grand Cayman)
Coolman-Ali, Tricia (Grand Cayman)
Costello, Elissa (Grand Cayman)
Dauphinee, Anne (Grand Cayman)
Deeney, Angela (Grand Cayman)
Dickson, Jessie Anne (Grand Cayman)
Emmett, Isabella (US – Florida)
Flowers, Dara (Grand Cayman)
Francis, Sherri (Grand Cayman)
Freeman, Wendy (Grand Cayman)
Gaffigan, Debra (Grand Cayman)
Gavin, Claire (Grand Cayman)
Gibbs, Christine (Grand Cayman)
Gibbs, Ira (Grand Cayman)
Gower, Denise (Grand Cayman)
Graham-Taylor, Emma (Grand Cayman)
Green, Georgina (Grand Cayman)
Groom, Jill (Grand Cayman)
Hawkes, Anna-Lisa (Grand Cayman)
Hawkins, Erin (Grand Cayman)
Hedger, Kirstin (Grand Cayman)
Heiss, Janet (Grand Cayman)
Hew, Sandy (Grand Cayman)
Hoar, Josie (Grand Cayman)
Howden, Vicki (Grand Bahama)
Houghton, Lizzie (Grand Cayman)
Hui, Dayna (Grand Cayman)
Hydes, Celia (Grand Cayman)

James, Keisha (Grand Cayman)
Jeffries, Angeline (Grand Cayman)
Jensen, Suzanne (Grand Cayman)
Jones, Stephanie (Canada – Ontario)
Jones, Ann (Grand Cayman)
Jones, Philippa (Grand Cayman)
Karlowee, Freda (Canada – British Columbia)
Kato, Naomi (Grand Cayman)
Kerr, Susan (Grand Cayman)
Koetze, Martine (Grand Cayman)
Kulcheski, Faye (Grand Cayman)
Lacey, Catherine (Grand Cayman)
Last, Zoe (Grand Cayman)
Lees, Elisabeth (Grand Cayman)
Loupelle, Pamela (Canada – Alberta)
Ma, Alice (US – California)
Macken, Celine ((Grand Cayman)
MacRae, Anna (Grand Cayman)
Makus, Carolyn (Grand Cayman)
Mays, Maria (Grand Cayman)
McLaughlin, Christina (Grand Cayman)
Mesquita, Jeaneta (Grand Cayman)
McDonald, Erika (Grand Cayman)
Meier, Susan (US – Florida)
Moon, Jane (Grand Cayman)
Nehra, Samantha (Grand Cayman)
Nieuwenhuis, Joy (Grand Cayman)
Nolan, Alexandra (Grand Cayman)
O'Keeffe, Shevaun (Grand Cayman)
O'Reilly, Avril (Grand Cayman)
Pandohie, Marion (Grand Cayman)
Parsons, Nancy (US – Minnesota)
Poirier, Jeannette (Grand Cayman)
Ponce, Mandi (Grand Cayman)
Ralli, Antonia (Grand Cayman)
Reader, Jessica (Grand Cayman)
Ribbins, Laura (Grand Cayman)
Ridsdale, Catherine (Grand Cayman)
Rix, Jeanine (Grand Cayman)
Robinson, Gerry (Grand Cayman)
Rochester, Michele (Grand Cayman)
Rowe, Katrina (Grand Cayman)
Saunders, Ceri (Grand Cayman)
Scanlan, Laura (Grand Cayman)

Schvartz, Marisa (Grand Cayman)
Scott, Lucy (Grand Cayman)
Scott, Paula (Grand Cayman)
Seymour, Shannon (Grand Cayman)
Sharma, Reshma (Grand Cayman)
Sherman, Sonya (Grand Cayman)
Singleton, Vanessa (Grand Cayman)
Southgate, Sally (Grand Cayman)
Sowerby, Nicola (Grand Cayman)
Stang, Shannon (US – Minnesota)
Sutcliffe, Sonia (Grand Cayman)
Sweeney, Becky (US – Texas)
Thompson, Suzanne (US – Tennessee)
Thomson, Helen (Grand Cayman)
Topp, Sarah (Grand Cayman)
Toor, Bobby (Grand Cayman)
Touhey, Tracey (Grand Cayman)
Unick, Amber (Grand Cayman)
Van Vliet, Monique (Grand Cayman)
Watling, Susan (Grand Cayman)
Webster, Janice (Canada – Alberta)
Wille, Gina (US – Illinois)
Williams, Jennifer (France)
Wilson, Barb (Grand Cayman)
Wilson, Julie (US – Washington)
Wong, Gaynor (Grand Cayman)

2006 Cayman Islands Full Marathon Finishers

Women

Armstrong, Julia (United Kingdom)
Evins, Lyn (Grand Cayman)
Hansen, Anja (Denmark)
Hoepfner, Meng (US – Virginia)
Knox, Laura (Grand Cayman)
Kovach, Andrea (US – Illinois)
Lee, Erma (US – Texas)
Loyd, Joclyn (Grand Cayman)
Maglione, Gabriella (US – Vermont)
McLean, Angela (US – Minnesota)
O'Sullivan, Kathleen (US – Massachusetts)
Sanders, Trudy (US – Texas)
Schreader, Beth (Grand Cayman)
Schrader, Kimberly (US – Illinois)
Stackhouse, Julie (US – Florida)
Walton, Laura (Little Cayman)

Men

Adams, Ben (Grand Cayman)
Anderson, Malcolm (New Zealand)
Buehler, John (US – Florida)
Bulmer, Darcy (Grand Cayman)
Cerame, David (Grand Cayman)
Clayson, Paul (Grand Cayman)
Delaney, Kevin (US – North Carolina)
Efferl, Hannes (Grand Cayman)
Haines, Derek (Grand Cayman)
Hines, Tim (Grand Cayman)
Huffman, Richard Lutz (US – Florida)
Hydes, Mark (Grand Cayman)
Jackson, Stephan (US – Pennsylvania)
Keith, Curtis (Grand Cayman)
King, Dylan (Grand Cayman)
Kressner, Kevin (US – Massachusetts)

McCann, James (Grand Cayman)
McGeough, Paul (Grand Cayman)
McLean, Ross (US – Minnesota)
McPheters, Michael (US – Illinois)
Miller, Tadd (US – Indiana)
Nell, Rupert (Grand Cayman)
Nielsen, Jespes (Denmark)
Palavicini, Martin (US – California)
Rauschenberg, Dane (US – Virginia)
Ridsdale, Michael (Grand Cayman)
Stephens, Tom (Grand Cayman)
Stuyver, Marc (Canada – Ontario)
Southall, Jay (Canada – British Columbia)
Tigerstrom, Mats (Grand Cayman)
Torres, Eduardo (Canada – Alberta)
Turner, Matthew (Australia)

About the Author

Malcolm Anderson is a writer based in the Village of Yarker, Ontario, Canada. He is currently completing two other marathon books that will be released in 2007, 'The Marathon: From Athens to Disney', and 'The 100 Marathon Club'. He has written two books of humour: 'Frailty of the Humour Mind' and 'Humour on the Run: Unplugged, Unshaven, Unconscious' and one book of poetry. He writes other humour stories in addition to the non-fictional marathon writing. Malcolm has run several marathons and one ultra-marathon. He runs in size 10 asics GT-2110 running shoes.

Other marathon books by the author:

The Marathon: From Athens to Disney

This is the true story of 3 marathons and an odyssey. The Athens marathon is held in November each year. Home of the marathon, home of the legend. It is run on the original marathon course of the 1896 Olympics – from Marathon to Athens, finishing in the Panathinaikon Olympic Stadium in the centre of Athens. Two months later in early January, Walt Disney World hosts the Goofy Challenge – run the half marathon around Disney World on the Saturday and you get a Donald Duck medal. Do the Full marathon on the Sunday and you get a Mickey Mouse medal. Complete both, and you get a Goofy medal. To many people it doesn't get much better than that.

Unless of course, you decide to head to the Caribbean and run a marathon there. So the author did just that, with the flat and beautiful Cayman Islands marathon at the beginning of December. The Walt Disney World Goofy Challenge epitomizes the transition of 'the marathon' from legend and Olympic heroes to worldwide societal mainstream. The book is a personal journey. It is a societal journey. It traces the transformation of marathon running while at the same time being part travel-log, and part training as it details the successes and the dismal failures of training for these three events. (To be released in the Fall, 2007)

The 100 Marathon Club

In this book the author writes about the experiences of people who have run over 100 marathons. To most people, running a marathon is a remarkable and remotely possible achievement; a major lifetime accomplishment. To run 100 or more marathons is even harder to comprehend. Why would people run 100 marathons? Why have some people run over 300 and 400 marathons? Or over 1,000?

The experiences and stories of those who have run 100 marathons or more are fascinating. Their running has taken them all over the world, including marathons in the Arctic, Mt. Everest and Antarctica. They run for charities, for enjoyment, the social connections made, and to help others. They run dressed as Superman, or as a Polar Bear. They run for health reasons, to see the world, to regain health after heart attacks and cancer. They have a passion and a commitment. They are like you and me and they love running marathons. And they are a group of the friendliest bunch of people you'll ever meet.

The author has had the privileged of meeting and interviewing 100 Marathon Club members around the world. They come to life in this book. We learn about their experiences, running and planning for marathons, their travel, training, the social side of running, use of technology, humorous stories, injuries, costs, how they fit marathon running into the rest of their lives, and their favourite runs. And they provide a wealth of advice for people starting to run marathons. (To be released in December 2007)

For more information on these publications contact:
The Experience Publishers at **irn@sympatico.ca**
Telephone toll-free: **1-877-755-5155**

The Experience Publishers